Rabelais's Laughers
and Joubert's *Traité du Ris*

Pour tout rabelaisant

Rabelais's Laughers

and Joubert's *Traité du Ris*

GREGORY DE ROCHER

THE UNIVERSITY OF ALABAMA PRESS
UNIVERSITY, ALABAMA

ACKNOWLEDGMENTS

I wish to express my gratitude to Floyd Gray, John Arthos, and François Rigolot for invaluable aid in matter and expression. I am also greatly indebted to the Research Overhead Fund and its director, Robert H. Garner, Assistant Dean of the College of Arts and Sciences of the University of Alabama, and to Richard Thigpen, Academic Vice President, and Charley Scott, Associate Academic Vice President. Without their support the publication of this study would have been greatly delayed.

G. DE R.

Library of Congress Cataloging in Publication Data
Rocher, Gregory de
    Rabelais's laughers and Joubert's Traité du ris.

    Bibliography: p.
    Includes index.
    1.   Rabelais, François, 1490 (ca.)–1553?—Humor, satire,
etc.   2.   Joubert, Laurent, 1529–1583.   3.   Laughter.
4.   Laughter in literature.   I.   Title.
PQ1697.L3D4   152.4   78–15341
ISBN 0–8173–7610–0

Contents

Preface

BEFORE MAN SPEAKS, he laughs. The most human of signs, laughter, because its meanings can be as myriad as the feelings and perceptions of man, is also among the most ambiguous of signs. The comic artist and his counterpart the theorist of laughter deserve our attention perhaps more than any other writers: they lead us to this richness of sense and seem to teach us that the mechanism of laughter is everywhere the same but that the matter for laughter shifts with the movement of cultures and time. A better understanding of the humor that animates the Rabelaisian *persona* must lead us to comprehend better the human that is in man. Rabelais's laughers, we shall find, are not confined to Renaissance France; the work and the laughter that bear his name are a part of the ongoing condition and experience of man.

Rabelais's Laughers
and Joubert's *Traité du Ris*

Abbreviations

EDITIONS

OCL	*Oeuvres,* ed. Abel Lefranc
OCJ	*Oeuvres complètes,* ed. Pierre Jourda
OCB	*Oeuvres complètes,* ed. Jacques Boulenger
TR	Laurent Joubert's *Traité du Ris*

TRANSLATIONS

TUPM	Trans. Sir Thomas Urquhart and Peter Le Motteaux
JLC	Trans. Jacques Le Clercq
JMC	Trans. John Michael Cohen
FG	Trans. Floyd Gray

JOURNALS

BHR	*Bibliothèque d'Humanisme et Renaissance*
ER	*Etudes Rabelaisiennes*
KRQ	*Kentucky Romance Quarterly*
MLN	*Modern Language Notes*
MLR	*Modern Language Review*
PMLA	*Publications of the Modern Language Association*
RF	*Romanische Forschungen*
RR	*Romanic Review*

Introduction

LAUGHTER, WRITES V.-L. Saulnier, is communication.[1] The same is true of literature, and it is where laughter meets literature that our problem takes form. Yet interesting as the subject may be, current aids, both historical and literary, as well as philosophical, are scarce. Marcel De Grève's *L'Interprétation de Rabelais au XVIe siècle* treats thoroughly numerous historical allusions and places the work in its literary perspective, but his study does not deal with its comic aspects. De Grève speaks momentarily and very generally about laughter in Rabelais, seeing it as an expression of the humanistic *élan*.[2] He pursues the author's reputation by citing references to him and to his work by contemporaries. In one of his articles, De Grève stresses the gross humor of the *Pantagruel*. Using again the historical method of contemporary commentary, he concludes that Rabelais's first book was not taken seriously by the humanists, and that the silence (absence of commentary) over his following books was due to the tense atmosphere of the Reformation. The Affaire des Placards receives special attention.[3] Yet behind this historical silence, as De Grève defines it, are we to suppose that Rabelais's work was not arousing laughter?

Other scholars and critics, while elucidating Rabelais's various profiles, manage to throw little light on his boisterous mirth. The notable French historian Lucien Febvre probes deeply the religious questions in his remarkable thesis *Le Problème de l'incroyance au XVIe siècle*.[4] This both patient and impassioned study seeks to show that sixteenth-century ideology, marked by scholasticism and syncretism, differs widely from our own. Little attention, however, is devoted to laughter. One of the most knowledgeable of Rabelaisian critics, M. A. Screech, brings back to life several doctrinal and institutional clashes that furnish energy and matter for laughter. This scholar puts the modern reader on his guard against "erroneous" mirth: "Of course, much of Renaissance science is quite silly by modern standards. That is what makes Rabelais so hard to understand. Somebody is always dashing into print to say that Rabelais is 'obviously' mocking a belief when he is doing the very opposite—defending an opinion which seems silly now but which then seemed the height of revealed wisdom."[5] But Professor Screech rarely mentions the author's style through which this comedy is re-created. The distinguished scholar Raymond Lebègue has written an important article on the laughable in Rabelais's use of different levels of style popular during the Renaissance, but the principal study of the author's comic devices remains Marcel Tetel's *Etude sur le comique de Rabelais*.[6] The French critic and novelist Michel Butor stresses the difficulty of understanding Rabelais, warning all who dare cross the book's threshold in search of this humanist's complex *joyeusetés*.[7] One American professor attributes the author's humor to a lack of logic as revealed in some of the oral discourses in certain episodes,[8] whereas still another finds a partial explanation of the comic properties of the *Pantagruel* in its peculiar prose style.[9] What unites all these seemingly divergent approaches to Rabelaisian creation is their adherence to modern points of comic reference.

Still others diminish or suppress hilarity in the work to bolster theories that lie beyond the text. At one point in his *Rabelais au futur*, for example, Jean Paris neglects the context laughter helps structure by eliminating it from the passages he cites.[10] Indeed, too little has been said by critics about the extent to which laughter animates the novel and to what degree this hilarity corresponds to sixteenth-century theories and categories of the laughable. We also note that three prominent literary scholars, Leo Spitzer, Raymond Lebègue, and Henri Peyre, have expressed the need for further exploration of the subject.[11]

A recent response is Professor Thomas M. Greene's *Rabelais: A Study in Comic Courage*.[12] This book offers an interesting presentation and interpretation of Rabelais, but it avoids the problem of the comic in spite of its title. Professor Greene is more intent upon showing the sardonic and ironic side of Rabelais underneath the work's gaiety, finally emphasizing the author's courage rather than his mirth. Other works dealing more specifically with laughter in Rabelais are Charles Hertrich's *Le Rire de Rabelais et le sourire de son pantagruélisme* and Ronald de Carvalho's series of informal essays entitled *Rabelais et le rire de la Renaissance* of which only a few paragraphs treat the subject of laughter.[13] A recently translated work by Mikhail Bakhtin, *Rabelais and His World*, opens a new avenue in Rabelaisian criticism because of its fresh vision and completeness in its proposed method; nonetheless it leaves an important dimension unmeasured with respect to our subject. This Russian critic speaks of the medical and philosophical sources of physiological theories of laughter and even mentions the *Traité du Ris* as representative of the contemporary awareness of laughter's therapeutic value. Unfortunately, he then turns his attention with such intensity upon the folk sources, images, and expressions of carnival laughter that he fails to take up the analysis of Laurent Joubert's treatise and its application to Rabelais.[14]

Literature on Rabelais is, then, despite these works and the important chapters by Paul Stapfer, Jean Plattard, and Pierre Villey on the comic, far from rich in studies on the nature of Rabelaisian laughter. John Cowper Powys in his *Rabelais* brilliantly renews and expands his earlier discussion of the author's mirth in light of today's attitude to hilarity, but we must admit that relatively little attention has been paid to sixteenth-century *risus* and *ridenda*.[15]

Joubert's *Traité du ris*

Although a host of authors have investigated laughter over the centuries, its causes and its effects, its circumstances and its meaning, Joubert synthesizes many of them in his treatise.[16] He is the most articulate theoretician of laughter and the comic in France during the Renaissance, spending possibly twenty-five years in arriving at an explanation of the phenomenon of laughter as complete and as integrated to the period as could be hoped by any student of intellectual history. Thus Joubert's *Traité* would provide a valuable point of reference for discussing the laughter in Rabelais's comic creation.

Specialists have been aware of the treatise since as early as 1928 when the French literary scholar Jean Plattard made reference to it in his biography of Rabelais, but it received no real attention until Bakhtin mentioned it once again as a possible source or expression of Rabelais's philosophy of laughter.[17] Bakhtin also mentions the existence of an earlier edition of Joubert's treatise, but gives no further bibliographical information. M. A. Screech and Ruth Calder suggest in a recent article not only the importance of the *Traité du Ris,* giving a few examples of its applicability to Rabelais, but also "recall that Joubert wrote his treatise in Latin but published it in French."[18] The French physician and historian Louis Dulieu fills many of the lacunae in our information on the composition and publication of the *Traité.* According to Dulieu, Joubert began composing his treatise as early as 1552—the year in which Rabelais ended the twenty-year publication span of his four unquestionably authentic books. A first version appeared, so it would seem, in Lyons: *Traité des causes du ris et tous ses accidents* by M.

Laurens Joubert, Valentinois (translated in French by M. Loys Papon, Lyon: J. de Tournes, 1560). This edition, suggesting an earlier Latin version, was supposedly published by his friends. Neither of these editions has yet been found. The only editions known to date, either in Paris or Montpellier, were published by Nicolas Chesneau in 1579.[19]

As for the author, Laurent Joubert was the object of a careful bibliobiographical study in 1814.[20] A brief *vita* will suffice here. He was born in Valence (Dauphiné) on December 16, 1529, and was probably educated in his native city. At the age of twenty-one he went to Montpellier to study medicine. He became the student of Guillaume Rondelet, the famous doctor and professor whom readers of Rabelais know as "Rondibilis." Joubert became a great educator; the students at Montpellier petitioned for his professorship upon Rondelet's death in 1566. He was later appointed chancellor of the Faculté de Médecine, *premier médecin* of Catherine de' Medici, and finally *médecin ordinaire du roi*. Besides the *Traité du Ris*, Joubert wrote numerous works in Latin, published others in French, among which figure Guy de Chauliac's *Grande Chirurgie* and his own *Erreurs populaires*—the subject of no small scandal inasmuch as he spoke openly of marriage and, what was worse, revealed in the vulgar tongue many medical secrets previously kept in Latin. He died in the small village of Lombers on October 21, 1582, not far from Montpellier.

Problem and Method

With Joubert's legacy of laughter in theory in one hand, we need not search for a counterpart in comic practice. It has long been well established that Rabelais looms, giantlike, as one of the greatest storehouses of Renaissance laughter. The novel contains both laughers and situations recalling the types of laughter and categories of the laughable in Joubert's treatise. Yet before confrontation can be legitimately executed, another problem must be faced: the reliability of Joubert.

The *Traité du Ris* is not well known among scholars of Renaissance letters. Only recently have reprints become available, and intentions of preparing a critical edition of the treatise been announced. Thus literature devoted to theories of laughter and the comic has not sufficiently taken into account the presence and significance of Joubert's theory or the validity of his categories. The first step, therefore, will be how to test Joubert.[21]

Although an inventory of the comic theories of the time will show that Joubert participates in the thought and beliefs common to his age, it will not leave his treatise any less an unverified abstraction or, obviously, Rabelais's comic practice better defined. The difficulty in determining an author's comic prowess through a purely literary study usually manifests itself on the level of method.[22] In discussing a given text, general ideas, particularly modern ones, such as Henri Bergson's, are inevitably used. Any attempt to describe Rabelaisian humor with more precision than a modern appreciation of the work is able to afford must approach the question not only from the literary but also from the historical viewpoint. This means our method cannot be one of simple confrontation, finding parallels between Joubert's conception and comic practice in the novel. Even though the four books of Rabelais enjoy worldwide renown as comic literature, we may not use episodes and sayings in his work initially for the purpose of assaying Joubert's theory and categories. Such a first movement would defeat the present endeavor, which is to ascertain more exactly the sixteenth-century idea of the laughable, since it would ultimately be based once again upon a modern judgment of the work's comical virtues in choosing portions of it for discussion.

However incomplete the operation might be, the more rigorous method of sounding out Joubert's system solely with occurrences of laughter in Rabelais must be adopted. *Textual laughter* is the term used in the present study to designate such occurrences of actual mirth, either in narration or in direct or indirect discourse. As the merry band celebrates Pantagruel's judgment on the difference between two lords in the fourteenth chapter of the *Pantagruel,* for example, Panurge plays with words in relating the effect the giant's shadow has on his thirst. The crowd's reaction to the joke is registered textually in the narration: "At these words, the company burst into laughter."[23] We know also that Panurge laughed along with the others in this particular incident; this fact is revealed through the words of Pantagruel, " 'Panurge, what is that which moves you to laugh so?' "[24] More striking is actual hilarity reproduced in direct discourse: " 'Ho, ho, ha, ha, ha,' said Pantagruel."[25] To all of these will be applied the term *textual laughter.*

The confrontation of Joubert's categories with textual laughter in Rabelais will provide a solid basis for further discussion. If a great number of them are corroborated, the remaining small number of unsubstantiated categories may also be supposed effective, by virtue of the general validity of the treatise and relative scarcity of occurrences of textual laughter in Rabelais. Once Joubert's categories are seen to provoke or accompany mirth in the novel, they may be applied to similar situations in the work where, for reasons we shall also discuss, textual laughter is absent. Joubert could eventually be used to evaluate other Renaissance works still less garnished with such laughter, thus determining their contemporary comic weight.

One might ask if we are not creating a false problem. Is there that much difference between our comic norms and those of the Renaissance? We are not alone in making our assertion. Our measuring stick, *notre aune,* as Lucien Febvre calls it, is not that of the sixteenth century.[26] If we see things differently, our laughter must also differ. When the as-yet-unfinished studies on the history of laughter and comic theory are completed, the determination of the quantity of comical Renaissance literature in France and the density of its laughter may be undertaken. At this precise future point, the conclusions of the present study will play their part in a clearer definition of the nature of Rabelaisian humor. The degree to which it was typical or an anomaly will be ascertainable. Such studies, by historical perspective, will also enlighten our present ideas on laughter, its functions, and its meanings.

In the meantime, Joubert and Rabelais may be studied, each in the light of the other's achievement. There is before us the unsolvable problem of the distance between the historical reality of the time and the unreality depicted in Renaissance fiction. That is, there is the lack of continuity between a real man actually laughing for a given reason or reasons in the sixteenth century and a character who laughs in a novel of the time. This method is, therefore, circumscribed by the degree to which characters are thought or not thought to portray the people of the period in which literary works are written. Tradition is one reason that justifies the use of fiction in formulating theory. Philosophers of laughter and the comic have traditionally gone to literature for documentation of studies and theories. Bergson, we recall, used the plays of Molière for his essay on laughter. Aristotle, in composing his *Poetics,* cited the dramas of the Greek playwrights to illustrate the essentials of comedy and tragedy. Thus fiction has always nourished principles; it can often be truer than fact.

Fortunately, for our purposes, the four books of Rabelais afford a variety of laughers ranging from giants—although quite human at times—to crowds, philosophers, and servants; all of these are valuable measures of what made people laugh. In short, practically all levels of society are represented.[27] If one admits that these characters reflect to a great extent the contemporary conceptions, beliefs, and customs, our method is reliable. Admittedly, there remains an unsounded gap separating the fictitious reader from the real reader and the historical author from the fictitious author; it is the dichotomy between art and life. Laughter is one of the bridges Rabelais builds in his novel to help appreciate the distance—or lack of it—between them. It becomes a way to see, feel, and hear the awesome resonance drawing both together: man himself, "for laughter is the essence of mankind."

Other reasons that make Joubert a good touchstone are mainly literary. The theorist furnishes a list of epithets of laughter that will permit us to examine in more detail Rabelais's laughers. Still more interesting is his expression of general theory and categories of the laughable; here we find certain traits that correspond with habits of thought and writing in the novelist's creation, helping us acquire a contemporary vision of Rabelais's work. It is this vision that makes more clear, after four centuries, Rabelais's meaning.

It is not, then, a matter of arguing for Rabelais's dependence upon a particular theorist. The objective is to understand the basis, even the underlying system of ideas in Joubert's exhaustive treatise. With this knowledge at our disposition we shall be able to elicit from Rabelais's work the notion of a system of laughter that will be more clearly understood, both in itself and in its parts, by confronting it with Joubert.

Sixteenth-Century Language and Thought: Meaning

Rabelais was well aware of the nature of these stumbling blocks, as can be seen in chapter ten of the *Gargantua*, "What the Colors White and Blue Signify." But this Renaissance Democritus wore the boots of a giant; what was play for him may be catastrophe for us. These hard facts must be kept in mind. Many terms are in a constant state of flux with respect to form and meaning. Accordingly, texts must be approached with much caution. The meanings of some words have taken complete turnabouts. In our realm of discussion the word *risible,* for instance, which today means laughable, also had the meaning *capable de rire* in the sixteenth century. Nor were categorization and conceptualization practiced with the mathematical precision we have come to take for granted.[28]

This last point is demonstrated by the meaning of the word *nom* as used by Pierre de La Ramée in his *Gramere* and Robert Estienne in his *Traicté de la Grammaire Françoise:* the term applies both to nouns and adjectives. Present approaches to language avoid such globalization; it has become second nature for us to distinguish nouns from adjectives.[29]

An example of differences in conceptualization may be sought in Rabelais. Principles were conceived of as agents acting in some mysterious way to accomplish their effects; a sympathetic internal law would have everything reassume its former place. Far be it from the Renaissance mind to visualize the ejection of cannon balls from the mouth of a *faulconneau de bronze* in terms of tremendous pressure generated by the explosion of gunpowder:

> Gaster put a flame to the touch-hole, thus setting fire to the powder. This at once exploded, projecting the ball and pellets with incredible force out of the cannon's muzzle, so that the air might penetrate into its chamber. Had this not occurred, the cannon's chamber would have been a vacuum. Now nature will not tolerate a vacuum: the machine of the universe—earth, sea, sky and air—would return to primitive chaos, before it admitted the slightest void.[30]

The unfailing principle responsible here is *natura abhorret vaccuum.* Nature refuses to bear the existence of a vacuum anywhere in the world; air must have immediate access into the firing chamber *because* the burned-up powder left an empty space. The load is expelled with great violence not because several atmospheres of pressure drive it from the bore of the cannon, but "lest the mountings of the entire cosmos, sky, air, earth, and ocean, be reduced to precreation chaos" over the persistence of a vacuum in the intimacy of an anonymous heavy piece. The forces of nature are less explained than they are enumerated, less questioned than imitated. Reasons are not sought but copied and then illustrated.

Such conceptions of natural phenomena, and such expressions of these conceptions, are both amusing and inhabitual for us. Yet familiarization with these differences will help us better to understand certain aspects of sixteenth-century laughter that now lie in the peripheral blur of a more modern logical focus. We must not lose sight of the mind of the period in pursuing the logic of the laughable in a century other than our own. Joubert will supply us with a means of comprehending laughter and laughing-matter. Although we today may find his conception curious and unrefined, studying it will reward richly the patience and the extra mental effort spent working in the Renaissance medium. Eyes, ears, all the senses, as well shall now witness with Joubert, permit us to attend the Rabelaisian feast of mirth.

SCHOLARS HAVE INVARIABLY approached the comic aspects of Rabelais's work armed with the Bergsonian theory of laughter.[1] Their studies, besides demonstrating the novel's comic worth today, confirm the value of Bergson's principles. Yet still other theories might be bolstered by Rabelais's practice, particularly one from the same Renaissance milieu: Laurent Joubert's, as put forth in his *Traité du Ris*.

His theory comes from a century during which physiology and a general concern for the corporeal side of man rose to new heights. Although the major mood in France from 1515 to 1530 was one of enthusiasm in art, letters, and commerce, the grim upsurge of the Reformation soon caused attention to polarize elsewhere. Many of the literary genres of the time reveal Renaissance man's frequent focus on his own body. The medical and philosophical treatises are no exception, nor, it will be seen, is the *Traité du Ris*.

The principal difference between Bergson and Joubert is that the former is more concerned with the psychology of laughter, as is the case with most modern theorists, whereas his sixteenth-century predecessor is concentrating mainly on the mechanics of the phenomenon. Bergson's comic theory carries the imprint of an age in which the machine, perfected by the industrial revolution, weighed heavily on an awakened social consciousness. The theory of Joubert, on the other hand, seeks to reconcile Aristotelian notions and certain medical beliefs common to the period. Both men, however, ultimately interpret for and to their respective centuries the source and the function of laughter. Both want to relate its meaning.

Before discussing the general theory expressed in the *Traité du Ris*, a brief summary of the "Indice des Matieres" will serve to reveal the overall nature of the work. Aside from the dedicatory *epitre* addressed to Marguerite de France, liminal poems written by illustrious Renaissance figures such as Jean Dorat and Joseph Scaliger suggest the importance of the treatise even before the table bares the scope and detail of each of the *Traité*'s three books.

The first book deals with the causes of laughter and with all its *accidens*. A philosophical inquiry on the *matter* of laughter fills the first four chapters, and chapters five through eight consider the role of the soul. Next, for eleven chapters, the physiological mechanism of the act of laughter is discussed. With chapter twenty begins an analysis of the accidents of *le Ris* continuing through chapter twenty-seven, after which a *recapitulaciõ* concludes the first book.

The second book undertakes a definition of laughter, a listing of its types, degrees, and diverse epithets. In the first chapter Joubert criticizes previous definitions before presenting his own explanation. The next five chapters cover various problems of false laughter, which he defines, and the last is a commentary on the principal epithets of laughter. The last book is consecrated to problems and applications of mirth. Here questions such as whether only man laughs—and why, of what benefit is laughter, whether a sick person can be cured by laughter, and whether one can really die of laughter are all entertained and finally resolved. Thus ends the treatise *in se*.

Appended to the *Traité du Ris* is Hippocrates's epistle to a certain Damagetes, which contains the famous account of Democritus's laughter; Joubert's brother-in-law Jean Guichard, also a rector of the University of Montpellier as well as a counselor and physician of the future Henry IV, is the translator. A short "dialogue" on the degeneration of French orthography, notes on Joubert's own orthography, and a few congratulatory poems make up the final pages of the 1579 edition.

Beginning with the second chapter of the first book, Joubert provides us with categories and examples of the laughable. He imposes order by using the traditional Aristotelian distinction between the comic as it is witnessed, or the *laughable in deed,* and the comic as it is recounted, or the *laughable in word.*[2] Since most philosophers make use of this dichotomy early in their systems or inventories, this first division of all laughable matter is not of primary importance.

Of greater interest is the theoretician's manner both of stating this duality and of subdividing beyond the fundamental areas of *word* and *deed.* Joubert expresses this traditional dichotomy in terms of the senses of *sight* ("*la vuë*") and *hearing* ("*l'ouïe*"), grounding all that is laughable in action and in speech: "tout ce qui est ridicule, se trouue an fait, ou an dit" (*TR,* 16). The particular order and titles he proposes in the various subdivisions under each major heading are the elements affording a contemporary view of Renaissance humor. Listing objects, persons, and circumstances that provoke laughter, along with frequent examples, Joubert performs a sort of anatomy of hilarity. He traces and exposes its causes as he continues to dissect each segment of the "matiere de Ris."

The *laughable in deed* is again divided into two fields in Joubert's mind: there are those acts that come about by chance, "il faut que cela auienne sans y panser"; and those that result from purpose, or conscious elaboration, "ceus qu'on fait sciammant" (*TR,* 20). Five subdivisions nourish the category of chance happenings: a glimpse of *les parties hõteuses* ("the shameful parts") has the first listing; *le cul* ("the bottom"), accidentally exposed, follows; the third place is assigned to the *comic fall; error* ("deception") in one or all of the five senses constitutes the fourth subdivision; the fifth is a curious catch-all named *legers dommages,* ("inconsequential breakage or destruction").

Following the surprise type of comic situation is that of *willful concoction,* acts purposely done that cause laughter, "sciammant, & de pansee expresse" (*TR,* 20–21). Consciously perpetrated comic deeds involve either imitation or practical jokes. The concept of *imitation* for Joubert is essentially a matter of pretending to be the opposite of what one is. *Practical jokes* are those "tours que nous faisons pour nous moquer ou andõmager autruy, mais c'et de chose qui n'importe, & qui et an jeu" ("tricks we do to laugh, or to hurt another, but in unimportant things, and in fun" [*TR,* 22]). In these instances, rather than being a passive observer or a victim of surprise, the laugher has an active function in the *fait ridicule.* This consummates the major heading of *laughable in deed.*

Joubert also separates the *laughable in word* into two areas that were and still are traditional. The first is the use of words as a means to an end, as in narration; the second is the use of words as elements of manipulation, or wordplay. The difference may be expressed as laughter resulting from what is told as opposed to laughter brought about by the words themselves, or again, in Ferdinand de Saussure's terms, mirth over the *signifié* in contrast to mirth over the *signifiant*.[3] Joubert expresses this idea quite simply in terms of the senses of sight and hearing—the physiological framework so characteristic of his thought: "L' ovye ressoit des ridicules propres à soy, & d'autres communs à la vuë. l'apelle icy communs, ceus qu'on recite auoir eté fais & vus, qui durant la narration samblet etre deuant les yeux" ("The sense of hearing receives laughable things both proper to itself and to the sense of sight. By the latter I mean those which are recounted as having been done and witnessed, and which, during their narration, seem to be before our eyes" [*TR*, 29]). Narration, therefore, in a very broad sense, covers all the categories of the *laughable in deed* discussed above; but as a subdivision of the *laughable in word*, it splits into fables (animals) and anecdotes (humans).

Wordplay is the most unwieldy of all the categories; its subdivisions are lengthy and overlapping. The terms are neither exact nor stable, a characteristic of many treatises of the time. This complexity in the types and sources of puns can be noted as Joubert outlines their makeup: "La propre matiere des propos ridicules, qui particulieremāt se raportet à l'ouye, et de ceus qu'on appelle brocars, lardons, irrisions, moqueries, mots piquans, mordans, equiuoques, ambigus, & qui retiret à deceptiõ, de quelle fasson que ce soit" ("The particular material of laughable speech is drawn from *brocars* [squibs, lampoons], *lardons* [taunts, sarcasm, gibes], *irrisions* [derision], *moqueries* [mockery, scoffing, ridicule], and remarks which are stinging, biting, equivocal, and which spring in any way from imposture" [*TR*, 30]). Based upon scorn and derision, wordplay according to the theoretician is laughable only if the contempt remain light: "Leur commun geanre, & à quoy tous conviennet, et le mepris ou derision: laquelle etāt plus graue & de consequance, deviēt iniurieuse: la legere, demeure ridicule" ("All come from scorn and derision, which when serious and of consequence become harmful, but when light remain laughable" [*TR*, 30]). Other conditions color the composition of verbal creations: "Or il y ha mille moyens de rancontrer, qui naisset des personnes, lieus, tams, & auantures fort diuerses: & sont an propos deshonetes, lascifs, facecieus, outrageus, facheus, niais, ou volages & indiscres" ("There are a thousand

ways to make puns, based on people, places, periods, and diverse occurrences: and they take the form of remarks that are disgraceful, lascivious,
facetious, outrageous, untimely, naïve, fickle and indiscreet" [*TR*, 30]).
The material cause of puns is defined as no less than the figures of rhetoric,
of which Joubert lists eleven: "Leur forme principalle et, des figures
d'oraison, ou manieres de parler communes aus Poëtes & Orateurs: comme
d'amphibologie, enigme, cōparaison, metaphore, ficciō, hyperbole, feintise, allegorie, emphase, beausemblant, dissimulation, & autres que mettet
les Rhetoriciens" ("They take their principal form from the figures of
rhetoric, or manners of speaking common to poets and orators, such as
amphibology, enigma, comparison, metaphor, fictio, hyperbole, pretence,
allegory, emphasis [innuendo], beausemblant [form of allegory], and dissimulation, and others put forth by Rhetoricians" [*TR*, 30–31]).

Joubert devotes only three of his fifty chapters to the formal cause of
laughter. This in itself indicates his passing interest in this aspect of the
phenomenon. What perplexes this doctor philosopher most are the
physiological springs at work producing the sudden movements, *les soudains mouuemās*, of the laugher. Leaving the cerebral side of laughter to
theorists of later centuries, Joubert proceeds to analyze in considerable
detail the emotional and corporeal role in the convulsions. Although his
theory is among the first to be published in French at such an early date, its
allusions to—and borrowings from—other treatises written in Latin are
constant. Mentioning only a few similarities and differences with other
theorists such as Vincenzo Maggi, Girolamo Fracastoro, both of whom
were Italian, and two French doctors, Ambroise Paré and Nicolas de Nancel, will expose perhaps more trenchantly the idea behind Joubert's general
theory.

The influence of Aristotle on all of these men is perceived frequently.
Besides the organizing function of the Greek philosopher's thought in their
work, one notices his basic explanation of the comic. This influence, either
direct, from the recently revived *Poetics,* or indirect, from Latin versions
such as Giorgio Valla's (1498), or Averroës's paraphrase of Aristotle, is
embraced by Joubert, but not without some modification.

We recall that the laughable for Aristotle is a defect or ugliness that is
not painful or destructive (*Poetics,* V). In the second chapter of the *Traité du
Ris,* Joubert postulates two abstract entities without which laughter is not
possible: ugliness and lack of strong emotion, "laideur & faute de pitié"
(*TR,* 18). This dual *sine qua non* is immediately associated with two emo-

tions in man, namely, sadness, over the ugliness, and joy corresponding to the absence of "compassion." These two necessary conditions permeate all the categories formed by Joubert. The opposition between the two emotions is further characterized when the age-old commonplaces of Democritus, the laughing philosopher, and Heraclitus, the weeping philosopher, are applied to joy and sorrow (*TR*, 9, 36). According to Joubert, contrary emotions are at the very source of laughter.[4]

A similar conception of this is expressed in literature. Readers of Rabelais recall vividly the moment of mirth shared by Ponocrates, Eudemon, and Janotus over the latter's ridiculous speech, the bell-filled harangue that was delivered to convince Gargantua that he must give back the bells borrowed from Notre Dame cathedral:

> Le sophiste n'eut si toust achevé que Ponocrates et Eudemon s'esclafferent de rire tant profondement que en cuidèrent rendre l'ame à Dieu.... Ensemble eulx commença rire Maistre Janotus, à qui mieulx mieulx, tant que les larmes leurs venoient es yeux.... En quoy par eulx estoyt Democrite heraclitizant et Heraclyte democritizant representé.

> The sophist had no sooner finished than Ponocrates and Eudemon burst out laughing so hard that they thought that they were going to give up the ghost, ... Master Janotus began to laugh too, and they all laughed so much that their eyes watered.... Here was a fine example of Democritus heraclitizing, and Heraclitus democratizing.[5]

Rabelais renders the throes of laughter with an oxymoron and engages the Greek philosophers in an antitheton to capture the throbbings. Several other figures may be seen at work in this heaving clause, but the important point here is that both the theorist and the practitioner see the same fundamental antonymy involved in laughter; Joubert explains it, Rabelais depicts it.

But this idea was not shared by another famous Frenchman and surgeon of the time. Ambroise Paré relegates laughter to a single emotional field: "L'affection risifique donc est mise sous la passion nomee joye."[6] Few of the contemporary theorists had this absolute conception of laughter. It is perhaps not without cause that the French historian Lucien Febvre calls Paré one of the most independent men of his time.[7]

Girolamo Fracastoro, however, strikes more than one familiar note with

Joubert's conception in his *De sympathia et antipathia rerum* (1546). Fracastoro holds that *admiratio* mixes with *laetitia* to produce laughter. This resembles the combination of emotions Joubert propounds. Joubert proclaims his esteem for Fracastoro and for other Renaissance scholars and doctors writing on the subject, such as Jules-César Scaliger, Jérôme Cardan, and François Valleriole; yet at the same time he emphasizes his independence and originality. Insisting he had been planning his own treatise long before seeing their works, Joubert states that he borrows nothing from them, trying all the while to do better: "Ie m'etois proposé cet oeuure, auant que voir leurs ecris: & depuis y mettant la main, ie n'ay rien amprunté du leur, ne methode, ne inuanciõ, pour y auenir (si ie peus) de moy-mesme, an essayant de faire mieus" ("I had planned to do this work before having seen their writings, and, in putting my hand to it since that time, I have borrowed nothing from them, neither method nor argument, in order to arrive at it myself [if I am able], all the while trying to do better" [*TR,* 14]). The question is not to decide whose explanation is better, but to single out the critical difference between the theories of these men who knew one another's works. Fracastoro, we have seen, conceives of laughter as the compounding of *laetitia* and *admiratio* but sees in this union an inherent danger for the *anima* of the laugher, since the former emotion dilates the soul and the latter suspends it.[8]

Before observing the precise point of difference in Joubert's theory with respect to this idea, it would be profitable to consider briefly the conception of another Italian theorist, Vincenzo Maggi, whose *De ridiculis* (1550) falls between Fracastoro and Joubert. Maggi also believes that mixed emotions are the cause of laughter, but like Fracastoro, he claims that the conflict takes place *in mente.* His idea of laughter remains that of a "motion of the mind."[9] Even though he knows that the heart and diaphragm animate the phenomenon, too respectful of the recently promulgated—and vulgarized—doctrine of Plato, Maggi is unable to say that laughter is anything other than a struggle between mind and body.[10]

Joubert manages to overcome the difficulties these two forerunners encounter by using Plato, but in a more elaborate manner. Far from seeing a danger in the combination of contrary emotions, as does Fracastoro, Joubert maintains that such blending is not only harmless, but actually necessary for man's well-being. As for the physiological role of the heart and diaphragm, Joubert offers the most detailed explanation; he resolves Maggi's dilemma by setting the encounter outside the mind and in the heart.

The progression of Joubert's thought may be followed step by step even in his chapter headings. He begins by discussing what constitutes laughing matter: "Quelle est la matiere du Ris." Next comes the two-fold Aristotelian division between deeds and words: "II. Des fais ridicules / III. Des propos ridicules." The fourth chapter is devoted to a grouping of added thoughts on extraneous elements that condition laughter incidentally: "IIII. Observacions aus ridicules." The following chapter poses the general problem that causes much difficulty for most doctors of the time, namely, was the heart, brain, or soul the "cause des mouuemans du Ris": "V. Quelle partie du cors ressoit premiere l'objaet du Ris." Chapters six, seven, and eight are a partial solution. Joubert decides to explain briefly the soul's faculties from which all our actions proceed, "les puissances de l'ame, desquelles procedet toutes noz actions": "VI. Division des puissances de l'ame / VII. Des autres parties de l'ame / VIII. A quelle puissance de l'ame il faut attribuer le Ris."

By analyzing the soul's faculties, the theorist intends to find those to which all the passions might be assigned, whereupon, having shown which emotions govern laughter, its eventual physiology might be traced to the particular organs responsible for the phenomenon: "Lors, & ayāt prouué commāt le Ris, come accident, suit quelque passiõs ou affeccions, on ne doutera plus du principal lieu de son occasion, que nous voulons trouuer" ("Then, when it will be proved how laughter, as accident, is connected to a few of the passions or emotions, the principal area of its occurrence, which is what we are seeking, will no longer be in question" [TR, 45]). Here Joubert's powers of analysis bear much fruit. Using a reduced form of the traditional framework adopted by the "Physiciẽs,"[11] he classifies the various activities in man: "vegetatiue," "sansitiue," "appetitiue" (TR, 46–47). The emotions, Joubert concludes, belong neither to the brain ("*sansitiue*"), nor to the viscera ("*vegetatiue*"), but to the heart ("*appetitiue*"). Thus as did Plato, the theoretician assigns the principal emotions to the heart.

As this part of his argument draws to a close, he calls once again to the fore those two opposed emotions central to his thesis, joy and sorrow, stating their particular influence on the heart's behavior: "An la ioye il s'elargit souëfvemant, comme voulāt recevoir & ambrasser l'obiet presanté: dont avient qu'il epand d'allegresse son sang & ses espris. Par l'espoir il n'an fait gueres moins: car il y ha presque tel mouvemant à l'imagination du bien avenir, que du presant. La tristesse & la crainte, comme contraires aus precedantes, troublet le coeur de contraire fasson" ("Under the effect of joy it expands thirstily, as if wanting to receive and embrace the object presented, whence it sends forth joyfully its blood and its humors. With hope, the same is no less the case, for there is an almost identical movement in the imagination over some future good as over a present one. Sadness and fear, as contraries to the preceding, beset the heart in a contrary manner" [TR, 51]). No less than eight more emotions follow, each with its contrary emotion, all having either a dilative or a constrictive effect on the heart: "ioye, tristesse, espoir, crainte, amitié, hayne, ire, compassiõ, honte, effrontemant, zele, anvie & malice."

After the lengthy discussion on the parts of the soul, Joubert pronounces his contribution to the mystery of laughter. The "matiere ridicule" acts upon the heart in a precise way: "Nous avons declaré tout ce qui precede l'acte du Ris: c'et la matiere ridicule, portee au coeur par les tuyaux des sãs, & qui premier le touche: lequel emù d'icelle, et agité alternativemãt de contraires & soudains movemãs" ("We have pointed out all that precedes the act of laughter: it is the laughable matter carried first by the conduits of the senses to touch the heart which, in turn moved by the laughable, is stirred alternatively by sudden contrary movements" [TR, 90]). An important aspect of this notion is that the dilatation is longer than the contraction. The systole-diastole does not, therefore, enjoy perfectly equal time; its periodicity is composed of a weak systolic arsis followed by a strong diastolic thesis: "Le chacun [mouvemãn contraire] et court, pour etre soudain rompu de son contraire, qui lui couppe chemin: toutefois la dilatacion passe la contraction, comme an tout ridicule y ha plus de plaisir, que d'annuy" ("Each one [contrary movement] is short in that it is suddenly interrupted by its contrary, which undercuts it; still the dilatation outlasts the contraction since in all laughable matter there is more pleasure than pain" [TR, 91]).

How laughter comes from the rough movement of the heart, contracted and dilated in rapid succession, is finally revealed: "Le pericarde mù du coeur, tire le diaphragme, où il et attaché d'vne grande largeur aus hommes, biẽ autremant qu'aus betes, comme on voit par l'anatomie" ("The pericardium, moved by the heart, pulls on the diaphragm to which it is thoroughly connected in men, quite otherwise than in animals, as can be seen through anatomy [TR, 93–94]). Anatomy supplies the final link in the theory of Joubert. Observation proves that the organ surrounding the heart is firmly rooted in the diaphragm of humans, but such is not the case with animals. The pericardium, suffering the same heaving effects as the heart worked by the mixed emotions, shares its convulsive movements with the diaphragm. Thus, breath is expelled from the lungs in the familiar "ho, ho, ho."

Whatever our reaction might be to this sixteenth-century conception of laughter, one important fact is worth emphasis: Renaissance mirth, according to several theorists, and especially Joubert, is not the product of a single or simple emotion. It involves ambivalence. Also important is Joubert's mentioning the lack of a strong connection between the pericardium and the diaphragm in animals, thus reaffirming his close alliance to the ancient Greek philosopher who had claimed that man alone, among all the animals, laughs. For Joubert, as for most men of his time, physiology is a completion of philosophy. Anatomy was used to confirm established authority, such as Aristotle, rather than to confound it.[12]

Resuming the consideration of Joubert's chapter headings, we are now able to see how each one corresponds to the arguments of the day: "IX. Que le Ris provient d'vne affeccion du coéur, & nompas du cerveau" is addressed to a Maggi or to a Nancel,[13] for whom the first movement of laughter takes place in the head; the brain actually palpitates. Ambroise Paré is the target of "X. Que l'affeccion mouvante à Rire n'aet simplemat de joye." With chapters eleven through sixteen, Joubert's thought develops more independently of his fellow theorists' ideas: "XI. Ce qu'avient de la joye particulieremat. / XII. Ce qu'avient de la tristesse particulieremat. / XIII. An quoy conviennet la liesse, & le Ris. / XIIII. Que le Ris aet fait de contraires mouvemãns, empruntés de ioye & de tristesse. / XV. De quel mouvemãt le coeur se meut au Ris. / XVI. Commant le diaphragme aet ebranlé par le Ris."

Although Joubert completes at this point the exposition of his novel theory, he continues to give current ideas, reflections, and anecdotes on the subject for two hundred and fifty pages. The names he cites throughout the rest of his treatise are meant to reinforce his argument and its prestige: Plato, Galen, Aristotle, Aulus Gellius, Cicero, and Herodotus are but a few; sixty names are paraded before the final page is turned. Indeed, with the help of his contemporaries and predecessors, and by calling upon Plato in a crucial moment, Joubert manages to confirm on medical grounds what Aristotle had advanced in theory.

The *Traité du Ris* might seem to be a great document of the Renaissance, but the truth remains that its philosophical and medical erudition is infinitely overshadowed by the sheer comic genius of Rabelais. It is unnecessary to show that his comic practice has been a far greater staple over the centuries than the theories he himself or other men of his time might have held or developed. The task at hand is to draw the parallels that exist between theory, as Joubert states it, and the laughter, as the novelist supplies it. We may thus deepen our knowledge of sixteenth-century laughers and their laughter and our appreciation of Rabelais's enormous comic achievement.

Chapter 2

Chance and Surprise

THE ELEMENT OF SURPRISE depends upon a universe in which chance, although certainly not governing entirely the particular way reality unfolds in time, has nevertheless a recognizable role. The convolute complications the reader witnesses as he progresses through the Rabelaisian cosmos may never be equated with those complexities to which chance gives rise in real life. To speak of surprise in literature, then, involves a concession on the part of the reader or critic, "a willing suspension of disbelief."

We must, therefore, reassign chance to a particular level of narration in Rabelais's work. An obvious possibility is the first level, that of Alcofrybas Nasier in the *Pantagruel* and the *Gargantua,* and Rabelais in the *Tiers* and *Quart Livre.* Once it is decided that the duo constituting the authorial I shall represent, with words, phrases, and sentences, the moments, seconds, and minutes of a "real" world, accidents may happen once again, and a sudden, unexpected occurrence reassumes all its startling virtue. One of the consequences of choosing the first level of narration is the possibility of applying Rabelais's laughers to Joubert's five laughable instances subject to chance:

1. *les parties hôteuses* (the shameful parts)
2. *le cu* (the bottom, including buttocks and anus)
3. *la cheute* (the comic fall)
4. *la deception* (error)
5. *legers dommages* (inconsequential loss, breakage)

The Shameful Parts

Whether or not the order in which Joubert's subdivisions appear represents any sort of precedence is not clear. According to the theorist's listing, however, the first cause of laughter is seeing—accidentally—the shameful parts:

> Si on vient à decouurir les parties hôteuses, lesquelles par nature, ou publique honnesteté nous sommes coutumiers de cacher, pour ce qu'il est laid, toutesfois indigne de pitié, incite les voyans à rire.

> If one happens to reveal the shameful parts, which by nature or public decency we are accustomed to keep hidden, inasmuch as this is ugly yet unworthy of any pity, it incites the onlookers to laugh. (*TR*, 16–17)

The factor of chance is crucial; the theoretician maintains that anyone showing them purposely should be held reprehensible. Such an action is no longer matter for laughter: "les plus seueres reprendront aigremant celuy, qui deshonté les decouure à son esciant" ("the most severe will reprehend sharply anyone who unabashedly and knowingly exposes them" [*TR*, 20]).

Also evident in the example is Joubert's principal idea of ugliness and concomitant lack of emotion. He is very explicit about these two necessary conditions and imagines a case to illustrate this point. First there must be ugliness: "Si on decouure la poitrine, les bras, ou les piés, il n'y aura pas moyen de rire; par ce qu'on ne trouue pas laid, ne indessat, d'exposer à l'oeil ces parties-là" ("If the chest, the arms, or the feet are uncovered, there would be nothing to laugh at, because it is not considered ugly or indecent to expose these parts of the body to view" [*TR*, 17]). Second, any sympathy dismisses the possibility of hilarity:

Aussi le Ris ne nous surprandra pas, d'vne chose laide, suiuuie de com-
miseracion: comme si on veut oter le mambre viril à vn homme, ou maugré
luy, ou de son consantemant, pour euiter vn plus grand mal, il n'et possible
qu'on an rië, à cause du malheur qui ansuit vn tel acte: dont pitié nous
surprand & arrete, pour an déplaisir etonnés côtampler tell'operacion.

So laughter will not come upon us over something ugly accompanied by
pity, as the case of removing a man's male organ either with or without his
consent in order to avoid a greater evil. It is not possible that one laugh at
this, because of the grave consequences of such an act, over which pity strikes
us and arrests us as we contemplate in disgust such an operation. (*TR,* 17)

Thus Joubert's thought continues within the framework of his first example. The fact that *les parties hôteuses* constitute the first illustration of what is
laughable in a scientific treatise is an indication that a modern concept of
humor is not to be aligned systematically with Renaissance laughter. Nor
may we equate the state of the French language and customs then with
those of today. The main purpose here, far from repeating the worn but
necessary *caveat* that sixteenth-century humor was normally more coarse, is
to emphasize the still more basic, yet less accepted, fact: logic and language
were less tightly bound.[1] On the one hand to see reference made to "nature," to "*publique honnesteté,*" and to manners as reasons sufficient for
hiding the genitalia and on the other hand to see them occupying first place
as an example in a piece of scientific writing is nothing less than inconsis-
tent for the modern mind. But this also proves a point for the same modern
mind: visual possession of the genitals, whether by sudden exposure or
through an accidental glance, has high comic value in Joubert's conception
of the laughable.

There is a considerable number of instances in which the Rabelaisian text
emblazes in diverse ways the shameful parts. The frequent use of interjec-
tions such as *vietz d'azes* ("donkey-pizzles"), the lightning-fast exposures in
puns such as *et habet tua mentula mentem* ("that rod you wield has a mind to
it"), the old lady's fainting and falling down with her dress up, or Priapus
who stands up *rouge, flamboyante et asseurée* ("taking off his hood, and raising
his red, flaming, cocksure head"), or the *frater* who divests in front of the
congregation are but a few of a seemingly endless variety in Rabelais.[2] In a
very strict sense, the above examples might demonstrate the opposite of

accidental exposure; the writer eliminates from his art the factor of chance and the preponderant effects it has in reality. Yet in another sense, if one accepts momentarily that the narration performed by Alcofrybas or Rabelais-narrator equals the continuum of life, the role of chance is reinstated. Panurge's *maniere bien nouvelle de bastir les murailles de Paris* ("highly original way to build the walls of Paris") may then be reconciled with Joubert's idea of unintentional exposure: such an unusual proposal constitutes the element of surprise. Although the wall of *callibistrys* ("pleasure-twats")[3] is far from being a chance happening, it appears before the giant's imagination as a sudden occurrence, and he laughs: "Ho, ho, ha, ha, ha."

Other laughers to suffer such visual exposure are Gargantua's *gouvernantes* ("nurses"). The laughing matter is none other than the baby giant's *braguette* ("codpiece"). The nurses spend their time "à la faire revenir entre leurs mains comme un magdelon d'entraict, puis s'esclaffoient de rire quand elle levoit les aureilles" ("making it come up between their hands like a suppository. Then they burst out laughing when it lifted its ears").[4]

One is tempted to advance here Joubert's contention that whoever shamelessly exposes himself on purpose, *à son escient*, is reprehensible. Actually, no one is guilty of such an act in the particular case. Even by the theoretician's severe standards, Gargantua is innocent by definition since he is the patient. As for the nurses, they are pushed to hilariousness by what Joubert presents as foremost among the causes of laughter. But these handmaids are completely absolved when one realizes that in this precise incident the exhibition is certainly *indigne de pitié*, unworthy of pity. Moreover, to assign guilt is to avoid the question; the inevitable fact of laughter remains. Any preoccupation with the moral aspects of the exposure in the novel proves to be groundless when the uncovering of shameful parts is viewed as a *fait accompli* before the arrival of the *gouvernantes*. These attendants must be seen as the witnesses and not the perpetrators of the exposure, even though such is not the case in fact.[5] If we fail to see the giant's nurses as victims of an occupational hazard, we fail to see them in their true context. It is their situation in life that exacts from them their activities with the Gargantuan *braguette*. Their duties may be questionable by most standards today, but these women are acting in accordance with the customs of their society and time.[6] Of importance to the discussion is the fact that Rabelais has the nurses laugh at the unfolding *spectacle* and Joubert claims that such an instance produces laughter. Thus the theorist's first listing of the *Traité* and the example from the comic novel are in harmony; textual laughter confirms the *parties hõteuses*.

The Human Bottom

The second subdivision states that it is likewise unfitting to show *le cu,* which is, due to the ugliness involved, the very reason we laugh—provided excessive harm does not come from the act in question, for this would cause compassion: "& quand il n'y ha aucun dommage qui nous contraigne à misericorde, nous ne pouuons ampecher le Ris" ("and when there is no harm forcing us to sympathize, we are unable to contain our laughter" [*TR,* 17]). Joubert chooses to clarify this with an example that recalls Chaucer as much as it does Rabelais. It might prove to be helpful in reexamining those passages that the modern reader finds sadistic, for we have the case of one man exposing his bottom, whereupon another burns him with a red-hot iron: "mais si un autre luy met à l'impouruuë vn fer rouge de feu, le Ris cede à compassion" ("but if another puts a red-hot iron to him, laughter gives way to compassion" [*TR,* 17]). Since laughter gives way to compassion in this instance, we might think at first that Joubert is less harsh than he actually is. This becomes obvious when he qualifies the thrust of the iron:

> sinon que le mal-fait nous samble leger[0] [marginal note [0]Leger, comme s'il n'y ha chaudure, & que le mal n'y apparoisse.] & petit: car cela rãforce le Ris, voyãt qu'il est deuëmant puny d'vne sottise, & mal-plaisante villenie.

> unless the injury inflicted seems light[0] [marginal note [0]Light, as only a burn, and so that the hurt does not show.] and small: for that reinforces the laughter, seeing that he is duly punished for a foolish act, and unpleasant trick. (*TR,* 18)

It is by this last observation that Joubert allies himself to the Aristophanic notion that "pain is only funny if it is somehow or other deserved."[7] But to summarize, even if the example entails a small amount of suffering, the category is based only on exposure.

Readers of Rabelais are familiar with the scene in which the Sibyl of Panzoust *montroit son cul* ("showed her bottom"). What better example could the author provide for the discussion, we might say, than this elderly soothsayer who suddenly decides to turn about and show her bottom to the inquisitive band. Yet contrary to what might be expected, no mirth is generated by the incident for the characters involved. The precise reason for the absence of laughter among Panurge's company before *le trou de la Sibylle* ("the Sibyl's hole") is to be sought in the intense emotional climate. Panurge is frightened as he watches and listens to the prophetess: "Par la vertus Dieu, je tremble; je croy que je suys charmé; . . . Fuyons. Serpe Dieu, je meurs de paour" ("By the power of God, I'm all atremble; I swear I am bewitched. . . . Let us run away! Holy snakes, I'm dying of fear").[8] Neither Rabelais nor Joubert would admit to laughter in such circumstances. The former had suggested the incompatibility of laughter and strong emotion in his *dizain* at the threshold of the novel: "Amis lecteurs, qui ce livre lisez, / Despouillez vous de toute affection" ("O friendly readers who peruse this book, / Divest yourselves now of every passion").[9] The theoretician, it will be remembered, had posited as a necessary condition the absence of passion ("faute de pitié" [*TR,* 18]). Thus even though the physical revelation provided by the seeress must have come as a surprise to the group, no textual laughter graces the particular occasion.

But if the characters are forbidden laughter, what of the contemporary readers? Should they not, on the other hand, be expected to laugh both by the theorist's and the practitioner's standards? Since *pitié, affeccion,* and *compassion* were arrested at the beginning of the novel by the abovementioned *dizain,* what could stop the Renaissance reader from enjoying the Panzoust Sibyl's sudden and literal *cul pardessus tête?*

The Comic Fall

This same demand for an absence of passion plays a key part in the third subdivision under chance happenings. Joubert lists third what Bergson will use as his first and probably most famous example of the laughable, *la cheute:*

> Par mesme raison, voyāt quelqu'vn tomber an la fange, nous an prenōs à rire: car cela est fort laid, & sans aucun danger qui nous tire à commiseracion: tellemant que tant plus indessante sera la cheute, tāt plus grande sera la risee.

For the same reason, seeing somebody fall into the mire, we laugh about it: for that is most ugly, and without any danger of commiseration: such that the more that the fall is unbecoming, the greater is the laughter. (*TR*, 18)

Joubert's treatment is earthier than his nineteenth-century successor's, for he chooses to have his subject flop in the mud, *an la fange*, rather than merely to stumble and fall. This holds true in a follow-up example wherein the hilariousness is supposed to be considerably enhanced if the individual suffering the fall is very dignified:

mais nous rirons sans comparaison plus, si vn grand & notable persōnage, qui s'etudie à marcher d'vn pas fort graue & compassé, chopant contre vne pierre lourdemant, tombe soudain an vn bourbier.

but we laugh beyond comparison still more, if a great and well-known person, who walks affectedly with a very grave and formal step, stumbling awkwardly on a stone, falls suddenly into a slough. (*TR*, 19)

What was simply mud must now be a quagmire to receive "properly" the great and eminent somebody.

Literal Plummeting

Joubert's examples call to mind the fall of the "bloated counselor," only one of the many targets of Panurge's comic wrath. The trickster had thrown a banquet for the counselor's pages. The purpose, as will be seen, was for his own pleasure at the expense of the servants' pain. He takes advantage of their absence to cut the saddle strap of the counselor's unattended mule *de sorte qu'elle ne tient que à un fillet* ("so that it only hangs by a thread"). Quite predictably, the forthcoming result primes laughter. The pleasantly surprised onlookers enjoy it more than they would *cent francs* ("a hundred francs"):

"Quand le gros enflé de Conseillier, ou aultre, a prins son bransle pour monter sus, ilz tombent tous platz comme porcz devant tout le monde, et aprestent à rire pour plus de cent francs."

Then when some bloated counselor or other has taken his swing to get up, he'll fall as flat as a hog before everybody, and provide more than a hundred francs' worth of laughter.[10]

Brought down boltlike to the level of the pigs, the counselor incites in the novelist's bystanders a laughter that the theorist maintains to be inevitable. The reason is simple: "Cela est bien laid, & n'a lieu de pitié" ("That is very ugly, and does not bring about pity" [*TR*, 19]).

Joubert dwells a moment on this particular point to emphasize his idea of noninvolvement by qualifying this last statement. The fall of a "grand & notable personage" is laughable, says Joubert, because no emotion is present. All would have been without mirth, however, had the victim been "notre parant, allié, ou grand amy: car nous an aurions honte & cõpassion" ("our relative or true friend, for we should be ashamed and moved by it" [*TR*, 19]). We can sense immediately the similarity between this illustration and the analysis provided by Bergson in his famous essay *Le Rire:*

> Signalons . . . l'*insensibilité* qui accompagne d'ordinaire le rire. Il semble que le comique ne puisse produire son ébranlement qu'à condition de tomber sur une surface d'âme bien calme, bien unie. L'indifférence est son milieu naturel. Le rire n'a pas de plus grand ennemi que l'émotion.

> Here I would point out . . . the *absence of feeling* which usually accompanies laughter. It seems as though the comic could not produce its disturbing effect unless it fell, so to say, on the surface of a soul that is thoroughly calm and unruffled. Indifference is its natural environment, for laughter has no greater foe than emotion.[11]

Many people today still attribute to Bergson the notion that pity and laughter are incompatible.[12] Still another theorist, Nicolas Boileau, recalled the inverse of this same truth to the mind of the late seventeenth-century reader: "Le comique, ennemi des soupirs et des pleurs, / N'admet point en ses vers de tragiques douleurs."[13] These theorists agree that our own concern alienates laughter, and as Joubert goes on to say, it would be even more horrible "si cela luy auenoit an grosse compagnie: & d'auantage, s'il etoit vetu d'vn tres-riche habilhemãt" ("if this were to happen to him in

a great company: and still more if he were dressed in very rich clothes"
[*TR*, 19]).

This last observation permits us to apply its positive corollary: if the
circumstances of a great number of people present, along with the *tres-riche
habilhemāt*, makes the fall of a person known by us even more painful, it
follows that the same circumstances accompanying the fall of an unknown
party should engender even greater hilariousness. This is precisely what
happens in the Rabelaisian example. The expression *devant tout le monde*
designates the numerous onlookers, and the counselor, evidently neither a
friend nor a relative of Panurge— his antagonist, rather—is qualified by
two adjectives, *gros* and *enflé*, which suggest his overbearing nature. In fact,
he represents admirably the stuffed shirt Joubert describes in summing up
his thoughts on the comic fall:

> Mais il n'y ha rien tant difforme, & qui fasse moins de pitié, que si ce mesme
> personnage est indigne du rāg qu'il tiēt, & de l'hōneur qu'ō luy fait: s'il et
> hay de chacun pour sa fierté, & excessiue boubāce, ressablāt à vn signe vetu
> d'ecarlate, cōme dit le proverbe. Et qui, voyant vn tel homme trebucher
> sottemant, se pourroit abstenir de rire?

> But there is nothing so deformed, and which inspires less pity, than if this
> same person is unworthy of the rank he holds, and of the honor accorded to
> him: thus, he is hated by each for his arrogance, and excessive hautiness,
> resembling a monkey dressed in scarlet, as in the proverb. And who, upon
> seeing such a man stumble stupidly, could keep from laughing? (*TR*, 19)

The urge to beam in the glory of our relative superiority, according to
Joubert, is overpowering.[14] Similarly, Rabelais's onlookers are unable to
stifle their laughter as the snap of a saddle strap sends the primped fat
counselor plummeting earthward.

Figurative Fall

Such is the case of the actual comic fall. But what of the symbolic *cheute?*
One might think of the *haulte dame de Paris* ("Parisienne of high degree ").
Although she is, by far, less detestable than the overstuffed counselor, her
high station with respect to Panurge makes of her an ideal subject for a

Rabelaisian undoing. Here only Panurge laughs as she finds herself face to
face with animal heat:

> tous les chiens qui estoient en l'eglise accoururent à ceste dame, pour l'odeur
> des drogues que il avoit espandu sur elle. Petitz et grands, gros et menuz,
> tous y venoyent, tirans le membre, et la sentens et pissans partout sur elle.
> C'estoyt la plus grande villanie du monde.
>
> Panurge les chassa quelque peu, puis d'elle print congé, et se retira en
> quelque chappelle pour veoir le deduyt, car ces villains chiens compissoyent
> tous ses habillemens, tant que un grand levrier luy pissa sur la teste, les
> aultres aux manches, les aultres à la croppe; les petitz pissoient sus ses patins,
> en sorte que toutes les femmes de là autour avoyent beaucoup affaire à la
> saulver.
>
> Et Panurge de rire, . . .

> all the dogs in the church ran up to the lady, attracted by the smell of the
> drug he had sprinkled on her. Small and great, big and little, all came,
> lifting their legs, smelling her and pissing all over her. It was the most
> dreadful thing in the world.
>
> Panurge made a show of driving them off, then took leave of her and
> retired into a chapel to see the fun. For these beastly dogs pissed over all her
> clothes, a great greyhound wetting her on the head, others on her sleeves,
> others on her backside; and the little ones pissed on her shoes; so that all the
> women who were thereabouts had great difficulty in saving her.
>
> At this Panurge burst out laughing, . . .[15]

This passage confirms a number of Joubert's observations. First to be
mentioned is the general idea of ugliness, explicitly expressed by Rabelais:
"C'estoyt la plus grande villanie du monde." More precisely, her *habille-
mans* are referred to, as in the theorist's illustrations: *vetu d'vn tres-riche
habilhemāt* and *vetu d'ecarlate.* A final similarity is the fact that there are
numerous witnesses; this factor renders the embarrassment more dramatic
"si cela luy auenoit an grosse compagnie," as Joubert puts it. Rabelais
expands this concept even more by placing the desecration of the Parisian
lady within sacred surroundings, *en l'eglise.* Perhaps more of the onlookers
might have dared a laugh had the primal scene not taken place in church on
the feast of Corpus Christi. Indeed, no sooner is the panting menagerie out
of church for the procession than laughter begins to ripple:

Tout le monde se arrestoit à ce spectacle, considerant les contenances de ces chiens, qui luy montoient jusques au col et luy gasterent tous ses beaulx acoustremens, à quoy ne sceut trouver aulcun remede sinon se retirer en son hostel, et chiens d'aller après et elle de se cacher, et chambrieres de rire.

Everyone stopped to see the show, gazing with admiration at the dogs, who leapt as high as her neck and spoiled all her fine clothes. For this she could find no other remedy but to retire into her mansion. So she ran to hide, with the dogs after her and all the chambermaids laughing.[16]

Even the novel's model of *sagesse, le bon Pantagruel,* found the whole episode *fort beau et nouveau* ("very fine and original"). Thus whereas Joubert only embraces the literal *cheute,* Rabelais's characters find the hurried slide of the *haulte dame* from high station to basic acts no less amusing.

Rabelais's practice overwhelms the theorist's insufficiently refined subdivision, but Joubert's general conception of the laughable and the particular category under discussion are corroborated by the passages. Not only the Aristotelian idea of ugliness is faithfully adhered to by Rabelais, but also the thought structures characterized by antithesis and oxymoron that nourish Joubert's idea of physiological laughter. The novelist uses these devices in his practice but pushes them beyond the theorist's margins. Just before registering the fall of the counselor, Rabelais has him execute an added surge upwards: "Quand le gros enflé de Conseillier, ou aultre, a prins son bransle pour monter sus. . . ." This dramatizes the imminent *cheute* by increasing even more the eventual distance the haughty victim will be dropped: "ilz tombent tous platz comme porcz devant tout le monde." In adding *comme porcz,* Rabelais lowers still more the negative pole. We have already seen how the *haulte dame*'s assault was intensified by consecrating the context. Both doctors knew well the mechanism of the comic fall and express it within the framework of their century's patterns of thought. But the *dame Parisienne* improves the theorist's subdivision by giving it a figurative dimension.

Error

Situations involving "deception" are listed fourth among the fortuitous events that, when witnessed, cause laughter. Joubert uses a striking—

albeit common—saying to convey the notion in a general way: we laugh *si on prend merde pour miel* ("if one mistakes shit for honey"). Error is in turn subdivided according to the five senses: *le toucher,* also called "l'attouchemant," the sense of *taste* both as "espece d'attouchemant & comme organe des saueurs," *la vue, l'odoremant,* and last of all, *l'ouye* (respectively: touch, taste as type of touch and as the organ of taste proper, sight, smell, and hearing [*TR,* 24–27]).

Mistake in Touch

Someone touching a hot iron that was thought to be cold is one of the examples given of a "misled" sense of touch. Another is the mistaken sense of touch of a person who falls through ice that was supposed solid. It must be pointed out, before one accuses Joubert of confusing his terms, that the theoretician is perfectly aware of the distinction to be made between mistake in perception and error in judgment. This is evident from his marginal note, "ce n'et deceuoir le sans (car il iuge bien de ce que luy et proposé) ains l'expectation & attante" ("the sense is not mistaken [for it estimates correctly what is presented to it] but rather the expectation and anticipation" [*TR,* 26]). Joubert nevertheless maintains this artificial and anatomical principle of division. He uses the five senses as categories with which he organizes his own concept of error.

TICKLING.   In this same spirit of loose logic, the question of tickling is discussed here. Although it may be argued that "Chance and Surprise" is not a chapter in which tickling is properly discussed, its presence here can be equally well defended since *le toucher* is immediately involved, and especially since Joubert himself does not use the category of touch in the section on purposeful acts that are laughable.

Twice in the novel, there is the implication that tickling causes laughter. A favorite activity of Gargantua as a child, among numberless others, was that of tickling himself *pour se faire rire* ("to make himself laugh"). Later, in the *Quart Livre,* another character, Ponocrates, *se chatoilloit pour se faire rire.* No indication is given in the text concerning the characters' success in bringing about the sought effect. In Joubert's opinion, tickling causes a laughter that is "batard & non legitime" ("bastard and illegitimate" [*TR,* 190]). He calls upon the authority of two great philosophers and doctors of the time to bolster his assertion:

Premieremant Hieronymo Fracastorio, & avãt luy Nicolo Florẽtino, tous
deus personages cõsumés an sauoir, ont estimé le Ris, qui provient du
chatoulhemant, etre quelque samblant & apparance de Ris, sans avoir son
vray titre & naturel.

First Girolamo Fracastoro, and before him Niccolò de Niccoli, both persons
consummate in knowledge, thought laughter caused by tickling to bear
resemblance to and to have the appearance of laughter, without having its
true title and nature. (*TR,* 191)

The problem merits two entire chapters in Joubert's second book of the
treatise (*TR,* 189–209). He finally concludes that this particular laughter
is *vraymant faus* ("truly false"). In the novel, although the reason stated for
the tickling is to produce laughter, the self-ticklers show no signs of
hilarity, nor is any contribution made in the two incidents to the hilarious
atmosphere of their respective contexts. In the case of the baby Gargantua,
it is but one of some seventy activities, lost in the list of the little giant's
pointless acts. As for Ponocrates, it is out of boredom that he resorts to
tickling himself; in fact, the context suggests that he does this inadver-
tently. Deep in distraction, "Ponocrates resvant resvoit, se chatoilloit pour
se faire rire, et avecques un doigt la teste se grattoit" ("Ponocrates was
dreamily brooding, tickling himself to make himself laugh and scratching
his head with one finger").[17] In the last analysis tickling has no major
function in the comic novel. Although the phenomenon exists and is both
mentioned in Rabelais's work and thoroughly treated by the theorist, its
connection with "real" laughter is nonexistent. In spite of Aristotle's conviction that man laughs when tickled for the two-fold reason that his skin is
fine and that he is the only laughing animal, these two doctors ultimately
concur on what was no small issue at the time: "Asavoir, si c'aet vn vray
Ris, celuy du chatoulhemant" ("Namely, whether it is a true laughter, that
of tickling" [*TR,* 189]). Rating neither on the level of Joubert's causes nor
on that of Rabelais's effects, tickling is not to be considered as a genuine
laugh producer.

THE LIGHT-HEAVY BLOW.   In the twelfth chapter of the *Quart Livre,*
Panurge recounts the story of "le seigneur de Basché" and the "Chiquanous" and the abuse of the ancient custom of playfully cuffing one another at
an engagement ceremony. The purpose of the mild tap was to help all

present remember the forthcoming marriage: "Des nopces, disoient ilz, des nopces, des nopces, vous en soubvieine" ("The wedding, the wedding," they cried. "The wedding, and this will make you remember it").[18] A brief explanation of the context is necessary for an understanding of the laughter that bears upon the "mistake in touch."

The "Chiquanous," as Rabelais calls the inhabitants of "Procuration,"[19] were royal officers enjoying freedom from personal assault by order of the crown. They were employed now and then by a monk, priest, usurer, or *advocat* who bore a grudge against *quelque gentilhomme de son pays* ("any local gentleman"). Roughly the equivalent of today's subpoena bearers in their legal function, they were also burly men, "gens à tout le poil," as Rabelais calls them. The reason for the latter quality will become apparent. Their objective was to incite the anger of the *seigneur,* in this case it is Basché, to the point that he does them bodily injury. Penalties of financial ruin and prison almost inevitably ensued since the king, due to recent insurrections, refused to grant pardons. The method most frequently adopted by the Chiquanous to provoke the local nobleman's wrath is vividly revealed by the *truchement,* the "interpretor":

Chiquanous le citera, l'adjournera, le outragera, le injurira impudentement, suyvant son record et instruction; tant que le gentilhomme, s'il n'est paralytique de sens et plus stupide qu'une rane gyrine, sera constraint luy donner bastonades et coups d'epée sus la teste, ou la belle jarretade, ou mieulx le jecter par les creneaulx et fenestres de son chasteau.

Master Bum-bailiff will summon him, writ him, insult him, and shamelessly abuse him, according to his brief and instructions. Then, unless the gentleman is as stolid as an ox and has less brains than a tadpole, he will be compelled either to punch the fellow and crack him over the head, or to give him a good hiding or, better still, to throw him over the battlements or out of the window of his castle.[20]

In the particular case under discussion, however, *le seigneur de Basché* decides to play a trick on the royal officer by requesting him to officiate at a staged engagement feast. Now given the custom of exchanging friendly blows, the Chiquanous could not hope for a better occasion: he has only to be a bit heavy in his remembrance taps. But Basché was prepared. He had ordered Oudart, the curé who also happens to be a *puissant ribault* ("powerful fellow"), to put on an iron jousting gauntlet covered with kidskin and to beat the king's agent mercilessly. The fisticuffs begin; needless to say, the "mild" blows soon mount to a frenzied extreme.

Two objections may be raised with respect to the inclusion of this episode under "chance and surprise." One on the basis that Panurge is the narrator, rather than Alcofrybas or Rabelais. Theoretically, this would eliminate chance since Panurge is narrating within the framework of the Rabelaisian cosmos. The justification offered is that in this particular episode, because of its length and complexity, the true narrator (Panurge) fades into insignificance as the episode comes to life. Illusion here becomes more important than reality.

The second objection stems from the fact that the laugher *performs* the deed, which, normally, should indicate treatment under Joubert's category of acts consciously executed to provoke laughter. The justification is that only the external aspects of the scene are considered here; the *farce* is examined for its comic virtue from the beholders' point of view, who happen to be laughers. Obviously, the episode is rich in laughable possibilities in other categories, particularly as it develops throughout the next four chapters (*Quart Livre,* XIII–XVI). These are recalled for analysis in other areas of the discussion. Strictly from the victim's and onlookers' viewpoint, then, the Chiquanous scene is considered here.

The royal agent's sense of touch undergoes no small surprise. Rabelais's detail of the bludgeoned officer's wounds is seven-fold and anatomical:

> Mais, quand ce vint au tour de Chiquanous, ilz le festoierent à grands coups de guanteletz, si bien qu'il resta tout eslourdy et meurtry, un oeil poché au beurre noir, huict coustes freussées, le brechet enfondré, les omoplates en quatre quartiers, la maschouere inferieure en trois loppins, et le tout en riant.

> But when it came to the Bum-bailiff's turn, they treated him to such a lusty hammering with their gloves that he was knocked out and bruised all over. They turned one of his eyes into a poached egg in black butter, fractured eight of his ribs, knocked in his breastbone, cracked his shoulder-blades in four places, and smashed his jawbone into three pieces; and all the time they laughed as if it were a joke.

What strikes many a modern mind as sadomasochism is laughable in

Rabelais. Admittedly, Joubert's example of a misused or surprised sense is not as exaggerated as is the case with the Chiquanous's suffering sense of touch; yet actual pain is incontestably part of the comic experience:

> On et samblablemant trompé an matiere de fleurs, quand on y cache quelque chose pointuë, qui vient à piquer le nez au premier rancontre, dequoy nous rions bien fort.

> One is similarly misled in the matter of flowers, when one puts in them something pointed, which pricks the nose upon first contact, at which we laugh most heartily. (*TR*, 26–27)

Many modern scholars argue that the humor of such a passage comes mainly from the repetition, the listing of qualifiers, and the exaggeration of the damage inflicted.[21] This is doubtlessly true for today's reader and perhaps, though to a lesser extent, for the Renaissance reader. But we must remember that such repetition, such long lists, and even what we call exaggeration, all characterize much of sixteenth-century literature. Joubert, for example, uses nearly twenty adjectives to modify an ugly old lady in his treatise, which is not to be classified as comic fiction. Precisely what comic value, then, are this repetition and *copiae* able to possess if they are normally practiced? We must turn to Rabelais and Joubert for another answer.

This same thrashing motif is greatly amplified by Rabelais in the immediately ensuing chapters. In each case the beatings are accompanied by textual laughter. The very purpose of the institution of the Chiquanous in the Rabelaisian world is to procure pleasure by inflicting ruin on another:

> Le seigneur de Basché . . . par chascun jour estoit adjourné, cité, chiquané, à l'appetit et passe-temps du gras prieur de Sainct Louant.

> The Lord of Basché . . . was visited every day, writted, summoned by the Bum-bailiff, at the whim and pleasure of the fat Prior of St Louant.

Mikhail Bakhtin emphasizes the carnival tradition and the folk laughter issuing from the theatrical showiness of such description.[22] This is certainly a valid point, but one that might be completed by suggesting that Rabelais was rich in his colorful and vivid depiction of the Chiquanous's wounds for another reason also.

We know that Rabelais must avoid arousing his reader's or observer's compassion. Both doctors stress the importance of the Aristotelian axiom. An answer Joubert supplies, and one that might help explain Rabelais's purpose in graphically recreating the sundry contusions, lacerations, and fractures in such expressive language, making them more terrible than they are, is to render their ugliness. Here, Joubert's theory is engaged and is also strengthened. Whether it be a question of the actual observers, or the Renaissance reader, disgust is aroused if they are interpreted as being ugly. This disgust, mixed with the lack of *affeccion*—precisely because the Chiquanous is the enemy, or at least the antagonist—engenders the laughter that Joubert predicts as physiologically ineluctable.[23]

Seen in this light, although the injuries incurred during Basché's performance are extensive, without them no laughter could animate the passages of the suffering Chiquanous. Both Joubert and Rabelais insist upon a mirth that is not absolutely painless; the theorist and the practitioner concur, albeit to differing degrees, that laughter is ambiguous, involving more than simple *liesse* (gaiety).

Mistake in Taste

TASTE AS TOUCH. The unfortunate glutton who sprays forth his mouthful of scalding soup has been victimized by his "misled" sense of taste *comme espece d'attouchemant*. Error is the basis for this *deception au gout;* misinformation paved the way for the sudden and unpleasant revelation of reality. Despite Joubert's citing of this example as laughable, there is no analogous situation in Rabelais convoyed by laughter. The discussion, scarcely opened, must therefore close on this unsettled subdivision, halfway between touch and taste, without confirming it. We should not be deaf, however, to the lingering note of pain: the laughter in the theorist's example is dependent upon a certain amount of suffering on the part of the comic victim.

Can one say that this particular distinction is too fine to be of use among the gross, hefty strokes of Rabelais's creation? On the contrary, the novelist has already proven the opposite to be the case with respect to the comic fall;

he carried the *cheute* into the realm of the abstract whereas Joubert's concept of it only embraces the concrete. This will prove to be true once again when we examine the notion of taste proper.

TASTE PROPER.   From the birth of Gargantua amidst copious "tripes . . . tant friandes . . . que chascun en leichoit ses doigtz" ("tripes . . . so appetizing that everyone licked his fingers") to the closing feast—"vrai Dieu, comment il y feut beu et guallé" ("Gracious, how they drank and feasted")—the joy of a satiated sense of taste far outweighs the grave moment in the novel when *deception au gout* is mentioned. None of the textual laughter fits the example given by Joubert of a disappointed sense of taste:

> Le gout aussi et trompé, quãd on fait manger quelque chose amere, ou d'autre mauuaise qualité, ayant toutefois apparãce ou couuerture de douceur & bonté.

> Taste is also misled when one has another eat something either bitter or otherwise of bad quality, having nevertheless the appearance or cover of sweetness and goodness. (*TR,* 25)

We must believe that this area does not constitute for Rabelais the laughing matter it represents for the theorist. Too sacred, or simply too necessary for the physiological well-being of his laughers, Rabelais does not allow the sense of taste to play the difficult role of a suffering faculty in order to furnish Renaissance laughter. The single occasion in the novel where taste is mistreated is done so contrary to the author's will. It is a question of symbolic taste as Rabelais speaks of the malevolent readers who not only refuse to drink his literary *vin,* but even go so far as to *compisser* his winebarrel. Here, in the prologue to the *Tiers Livre,* no laughter is registered. Anger is the watchword as he growls at the rabble, the *cahuaille:*

> Pourtant arrière, cagotz! Aux ouailles, mastins! Hors d'icy, caphars, de par le Diable hay! Estez vous encores là? Je renonce ma part de Papimanie, si je vous happe. G22. g222. g2222. Davant davant! Iront ilz?

> Get packing, you hypocrites! To your sheep, you dogs! Clear out of here, you canting cheats! To the devil with you! What, are you still there? I'll

renounce my share in Papimania if I can get my teeth into you. Gzz, gzzz, gzzzz! Off with you! Off with you! Are they not gone yet?[24]

Emotions run strong, and, as was seen above with Panurge in the case of fear (Panzoust Sibyl), both doctors indicate that an aroused temper is likewise no context for hilariousness. Thus only Joubert's restatement of the general Aristotelian axiom is reaffirmed here by Rabelais. Error attributable to an upset sense of taste is not a source of laughter in Rabelais. If *deception au gout* is to serve as a viable category, it must seek substantiation in other comical literature of the sixteenth century.

Mistake in Sight

Empty promises of visual pleasure cause laughter. Such is the case, Joubert maintains, when it is announced that we are to see a beautiful young girl. When it is clear that we are aroused, *tresaffecciones,* by the proposal, we are introduced to an antithetical fulfillment, a wrinkled old lady, "barbuë, veluë, frisee, borgne, chassieuse, enasee, punaise, puante, morueuse, baueuse, edantee, rogneuse, orde & sale, bossuë, tortuë, ecropionnee, & plus difforme que la mesme laideur" ("with one eye, a runny nose, a thick and kinky beard and under-slung buttocks, dirty, smelly, drooling, toothless, flat-nosed, bandy-legged, humpy, bumpy, stinking, twisted, filthy, knotty, full of lice, and more deformed than ugliness itself" [*TR,* 26–27]).

Disappointment along the lines of Joubert's example seems to be what makes Lasdaller laugh in chapter XLV of the *Gargantua.* Frère Jan's remark about monks "visiting" pilgrim's wives was only greeted by laughter on the part of Lasdaller, obviously convinced of his wife's powers of neutralizing concupiscence:

> "—Hin, hen! (dist Lasdaller) je n'ay pas peur de la mienne, car qui la verra de jour ne se rompera jà le col pour l'aller visiter la nuict."

> "H'm, h'm!" exclaimed Wearybones. "I'm not afraid about mine. For anyone who has seen her by day won't break his neck to go and visit her by night."[25]

The unworried cuckold is amused by the idea of the sudden disillusionment of anyone who sees in the light of day what might have been the object of his lusty visions at night. Strictly speaking, the example fits loosely into the category since in this case a particular agent does not actually announce Lasdaller's wife as being ugly or beautiful; nor does Rabelais spend the adjectives that Joubert felt necessary to list in such an elaborate *incrementum* to express the idea of ugliness. Here the art of Rabelais is brief: the fact that she is ugly, that disappointment is inevitable, and that the whole causes laughter is given in the above quotation. Thus the letter of Joubert's category goes beyond the Rabelaisian incident in its precision, but the spirit is upheld to the full in Lasdaller's imagination. The pilgrim's laughter confirms the value of the theorist's subdivision. The idea of ugliness and the structural vehicle of antithesis animate both the example of the comic category and the laugher's expression of the humor of a destroyed fantasy.

Mistake in Smell

SMELL PROPER. The sense of smell is also subject to error. "L'odorer et propremant abusé, si on luy suppose odeurs puantes pour suaues" ("The sense of smell is misled in a proper sense if fetid odors are put to it as fragrant" [*TR, 26*]). The best illustration of this in Rabelais is perhaps to be found at the very end of the *Quart Livre*. Panurge, having undergone a moment of intense fright upon mistaking Rhodilardus the cat for a devil finds himself in a most uncomfortable situation. Pantagruel suggests that he wash and change his clothing:

> "Allez, dist Pantagruel, allez, de par Dieu, vous estuver, vous nettoyer, vous asceurer, prendre chemise blanche, et vous revestir."

> "Off with you," said Pantagruel, "off with you, for God's sake. Take a hot bath, clean yourself, calm your fears, put on a clean shirt, and get dressed."[26]

But Panurge playfully seizes upon error, seemingly taking *merde pour miel*. The honey is, in this case, Irish saffron:

> "Ha, ha ha! houay! Que diable est cecy? Appelez vous cecy foire, bren, crottes, merde, fiant, dejection, matiere fecale, excrement, repaire, laisse,

esmeut, fumée, estron, scybale, ou spyrathe? C'est, croy je, sapphran d'Hibernie."

"Ha, ha, ha! But ho! What the devil's this? Do you call it shit, turds, crots, ordure, deposit, fecal matter, excrement, droppings, fumets, motion, dung, stronts, scybale, or sprathe? It's saffron from Ireland, that's what I think it is."

In a strict sense, the above example is valid in this part of the discussion only to the extent that Panurge is considered as the observer, and we shall have to deal later with Pantagruel's reaction to Panurge's predicament. Excrement, seen as a substitute of saffron from *Hibernia,* whether the equivalence is established on the visual level as saffron yellow, or on the olfactory level as Irish crocus, inspires hilarity on the part of Panurge: "Ho, ho, hie! C'est sapphran d'Hibernie! Sela! Beuvons" ("Ho, ho, ho! Saffron from Ireland! It is indeed. Let's have a drink"). The error is willful, but the effect is so sudden as to create the illusion of chance: Panurge laughs over the appropriateness with which a coincidence of language both embraces his situation and transforms his base state. Thus the windfall saffron metaphor sings Panurge's poetical error of *merde pour miel,* and his mirth confirms the category.

SMELL MORE GENERALLY. The sense of smell can be "abused" in a less precise manner also, *impropremant.* Joubert gives the example of offering a bouquet "parfumé d'euphorbe" ("perfumed with euphorbia" [*TR,* 26]). In this case the victim sneezes so violently and for so long a time *que c'et pour rire* ("that it results in laughter"). One can only think of the episode at the end of chapter XVI of *Pantagruel* wherein Panurge makes *quelque bonnes dames* ("some fine ladies") laugh when he shakes his handkerchief fully charged with powdered euphorbium under their noses. The sneezing fit lasts for *quatre heures sans repos* ("four hours on end"). The cause of laughter in this passage may never be limited merely to the sneezing; other contributing factors will be examined later. On the other hand, it is impossible to deny its partial role. The practical joke came as a surprise to the ladies, inducing laughter. The occasion corresponds precisely to what Joubert maintains in his treatise, and is therefore a clear-cut case of Rabelais corroborating in advance one of the theorist's subdivisions.[27]

Mistake in Hearing

The last and by far the longest subdivision under "deception" treats the sense of hearing. Joubert furnishes a less striking example to illustrate this sense "an erreur . . . comme instrumãt des sons" ("in error . . . as instrument of sounds" [TR, 27]): it is that of being confronted with a worthless song both in its melody and in its lyrics, but one that had been alleged "ioyeuse & plaisante." Here is a case necessitating the recall of the sneezing episode just discussed above. Rabelais does not limit his devices for laughter, as does Joubert, to one category at a time; on the contrary, it is to his advantage—and especially to the reader's—to draw upon several laugh-provoking elements to nourish a given incident. The scene mentioned in which Panurge makes *quelques bonnes dames* sneeze for four hours without respite may now be examined from the acoustical aspect.

Panurge surprises the ladies by supplying an exercise in counterpoint that is sure to disappoint the ear, but not the mirthfulness of the most refined of Rabelais's laughers:

Ce pendent il petoit comme un roussin, et les femmes ryoient luy disans:
"Comment, vous petez, Panurge?
—Non foys, disoit il, madame; mais je accorde au contrepoint de la musique que vous sonnez du nez."

All the time he would fart like a horse, and they would say with a laugh! "How you do fart, Panurge." "Oh dear, no, Madam," he would reply, "I'm merely tuning myself to the counterpoint of the music you are making with your nose."

Whether it be due to, or in spite of, Panurge's contrapuntal efforts, the ladies' laughter remains unstifled. That the entire episode lacks any verisimilitude whatsoever should not concern us for the moment. The essential here is that Rabelais calls upon the sense of hearing to participate in the actualization of laughter, whereas Joubert asks of this same sense a partial explanation of what constitutes the laughable. We must not attempt to decide upon the ladies' "deception" as real or feigned. This becomes ludicrous with respect to the scene's already exploded auditory proportions: four hours of nasal *musique* with an anal accompaniment in counterpoint.

CREDULITY.   Other illustrations of auditory "deception" clarify the notion of credulity, which includes at once hearing and the sense of sight. An analogous subdivision, *credulité* is mentioned under the sense of sight. Since there is obviously much overlapping in these parallel subdivisions—a witness often sees *and* hears—both are treated here. The errors pass through the perception apparatus and "echeet à la partie de l'ame qui fait l'opinion" ("fall upon the part of the soul which forms judgment" [*TR*, 27]). It is important to recall at this point that Joubert has not lost sight of the proper dimension of "deception" with respect to perception. This is evident in view of his repetition of the fact that the senses are never really deceived or in error: "Car les sans ne faillet pas à recognoitre leur obiet: nous rions seulemant de l'imaginatiõ faulsemãt persuadee" ("For the senses do not fail to recognize their object: we laugh only over the falsely convinced imagination" [*TR*, 27]). The five senses serve only as a means of organizing the types of disparities in the clash of present perception and past conception. This is not to diminish their importance. It is on the contrary to single out the preponderant use made of them at the time, not only in organizing the thought of Renaissance man, but also in following it into his patterns of expression.

Laughable *impostures,* or errors based on credulity, are split up into two groups corresponding to two basic emotions falsely and uselessly aroused: love and fear. According to Joubert, the lover who suffers from "affeccios vaines & sottes" ("futile and silly feelings" [*TR*, 28]) is cause for laughter. In nourishing his soul with *vains espoirs* ("vain hopes"), in giving himself up to melancholy bordering upon madness, and other emotions and actions that spring from the same affliction, he commits deeds that others will find laughable. Readers of the *Tiers Livre* think immediately of Panurge as he undergoes the torments of love's cruel visitation. True to Joubert's remarks on the comic fall, Panurge's close friends do not laugh, but the masquerade he dons as he pursues at length the answer to his *me mariray je?* ("shall I marry?") makes of him a public laughingstock:

Epistemon . . . remonstroit à Panurge comment la voix publicque estoit toute consommée en mocqueries de son desguisement. . . .

Epistemon began by pointing out to Panurge that everyone was talking and joking about his strange disguise. . . .[28]

Further ramifications are discussed later, but the validity of Joubert's category is clearly indicated here by the jeering laughter of the crowd.

Similar laughter is spurred by unfounded or "erroneous" fear. The theoretician calls to the fore those timorous souls "qui de pusillanimité sõt trop craintifs" ("who, out of pusillanimity, are too fearful" [*TR*, 28]). They dread shadows and ghosts. A rat makes them flee and the apprehension of being bitten stops them from touching a worm. Once again, Panurge's numerous manifestations of inordinate fear come to mind, both in the *Tiers Livre*, when he refuses to return to see Raminagrobis, and in the *Quart Livre* during the encounter with the Andouilles and throughout the storm scene. But his fear reaches the degree of paroxysm at the very end of the novel. Joubert speaks only momentarily of fear in his long preface to the second book of the treatise, but what he relates points directly to Panurge when he mistakes the cat Rodilardus for a devil:

> Et la peur, de quelle efficace la void-on quelquefois? D'vne soudaine peur, le trãblemant froid court par le profond des os, le poil se herissone, & la vois s'arrete au gosier: on se compisse, on se conchie. . . .

> And fear, what efficaciousness does one not see in it on certain occasions? From a sudden fear, a cold trembling runs deep in our bones, our hair stands on end, and our voice sticks in our throat: we bepiss and beshit ourselves. . . . (*TR*, 150)

The effects of this particular emotion, unfounded but nonetheless real for Panurge, are cause for hilarity in the characters who witness it. Pantagruel is seen to be unable to control his laughter:

> Pantagruel, le voyant ainsi esmeu, transif, tremblant, hors de propous, conchié, et esgratigné des gryphes du celebre chat Rodilardus, ne se peut contenir de rire. . . .

> On seeing his servant thus alarmed, shivering, trembling, bewildered, beshitten, and scratched by the claws of the celebrated cat Rodilardus, Pantagruel could not contain his laughter. . . . [29]

Although the modern reader might find Pantagruel's reaction somewhat brutal, especially in view of the distressing experience Panurge has just undergone, Joubert finds such a scene perfectly laughable since there is no pity aroused: "voyat ces mines, nous riõs de leur couardise (chose inepte & non pitoyable) quand il n'y ha pas matiere de vraye crainte" ("seeing these bearings, we laugh at the cowardice [an inappropriate thing unworthy of pity] when there is no justification for real fear" [*TR, 28*]). Thus, even some of the theorist's precise images apply in the novel, and the Rabelaisian scenes capture perfectly what Joubert says in diverse parts of his treatise on fear as it relates to laughter.

Errare humanum est is a commonplace. Aristotelian tradition carries another one of equal importance to our subject into the Renaissance: the laughable is caused by an ugliness that is not painful. Both are shared by Rabelais and Joubert. The latter fuses these two verities in the anatomical area of the five senses to generate his list of *erreurs ridicules*. Even within the restricted framework of considering only incidents marked by textual laughter in Rabelais, the consonance of Joubert's categories and occurrences of mirth in the novel, with but a few exceptions, is to be affirmed. The high incidence of examples and illustrations involving sadness, pain, and suffering indicate an ambivalent quality in the very nature of Renaissance laughter; here pain becomes relative to a period other than our own. In the sixteenth century, error and laughter are closely linked and seem to have a common source: it is in that which is proper to man, antithesis and oxymoron both in his thought and in his heart.

Inconsequential Loss

The last of the headings under which events governed by chance are grouped is dubbed *legers dommages*. People who "font grand'plainte de peu de chose" ("make great complaints over small matters" [*TR, 21*]) inspire laughter.[30] The reason for it is seen in terms of the Aristotelian axiom: "car cela est trouué laid, sans nous emouuoir à pitié ("for that is found to be ugly, without moving us to pity" [*TR, 22*]).

Chapter XX of *Gargantua* may be recalled in connection with this category. The episode is Janotus's famous harangue, which is a great deal of wind over nothing, since the bells—the subject of his pleading—had already been given back. Such disproportion between matter and expression contributes with many other reasons to one of the most celebrated outbursts of laughter in the novel:

> Le sophiste n'eut si toust achevé que Ponocrates et Eudemon s'esclafferent de rire tant profondement que en cuiderent rendre l'ame à Dieu, ne plus ne moins que Crassus . . . mourut de rire.

> No sooner had the sophist concluded than Ponocrates and Eudemon burst out laughing so heartily that they nearly gave up the ghost, exactly like Crassus . . . died of laughing.[31]

Epistemon and Ponocrates are aware of the futility of Janotus's empty harangue on the surface of the episode. But they may also be said to stand for man's awareness of the deeper hollowness of what Janotus represents. A. J. Krailsheimer speaks along these lines when he says that "Janotus is the pedantic fossil which all systems seem to produce sooner or later, and he is not more typical of Scholasticism than of any other system."[32]

Fossils are harmless, at least as Rabelais depicts this atrophied theologian. When the evil done is relatively small, and the perturbation is great, Joubert foresees a laughable situation coming into being: "La sottise est indessante & laide, le dommage ne merite cōpassion: voylà dequoy on rit" ("The stupidity is inappropriate and ugly, the harm does not merit compassion: there is what is laughed at" [TR, 22]). Both the general theory and the particular—although broad—category are confirmed by Rabelais's laughers in this instance.

The effect of the laughter on the laughers is benevolent. Eudemon and Ponocrates confer with Gargantua on the subject: all are swept up in a grateful and charitable urge to complement the joyous but empty harangue with something substantial. The sausages, having previously only a linguistic existence in Janotus's windy discourse, acquire fleshy fullness and become temporospatially real under the form of the laughers' gift: "on luy baillast les dix pans de saulcice mentionnez en la joyeuse harangue" ("he was given the ten strings of sausages mentioned in his jolly harangue"). Still other presents were showered upon Janotus, "veu qu'il leurs avoit donné de passetemps et plus faict rire que n'eust Songecreux" ("since he had so amused them and made them laugh more than ever the actor Songecreux did").

Joubert also alludes to the charity and other social graces and virtues that laughter can inspire when he speaks of the sanguine laugher, "l'*Eusarcie*, c'et à dire, l'etre moyennemant charnu" ("*Eusarxia*, that is to say, the moderately fleshy being"), as opposed to the melancholic "Agelaste . . . Apathes . . . Misanthrope" ("Agelast . . . Apathetic . . . Misanthropist" [*TR*, 260]).

Car les sanguins sont naturellemãt dous, gracieus, pitoyables, misericordieus, humains, courtois, liberaus, civils, affables, faciles, & traitable, hardis, amiables, accompagnables, & de bonne chere: dequelles cõdicions & vertus, le vray naturel de l'homme et naïvemãt exprimé.

For the sanguine are naturally gentle, gracious, compassionate, merciful, humane, courteous, liberal, polite, affable, easy-going and accommodating, hardy, amiable, good company and of good countenance: from which conditions and virtues, the true nature of man is genuinely expressed. (*TR*, 260–61)

In the eyes of the novelist and the theoretician alike, such freely giving laughers, perhaps because they are freely given to laughter, seem to constitute man in his natural state. Janotus, less generous, and overly submissive to the authority of the Sorbonne, remains *et croteux et morveux* ("both dirty and snotty"). Rabelais does not forbid him the pleasure of laughter,[33] but the *mervelheus effais*, the marvelous effects of this divine phenomenon, as Joubert refers to them, fail to touch the sophist's character or his health. Being a fossil, his laughter is borrowed. Merely an echo of Eudemon's and Ponocrates's genuine and self-generating laughter, it follows Janotus's inward convolutions to fossilization. His laughter, like the bells he represents, is so much sounding brass.

Summary

In the main, the five sections of chance happenings receive corroboration from Rabelais's characters. In some cases, where particular subdivisions fail to provoke hilarity, further analysis of the context reveals reasons that correspond to Joubert's Aristotelian conception of laughter as well as other related areas of the discussion in the treatise—such as fear and laughter. Lack of emotion is emphasized, however, and is to be restated by Boileau and Bergson alike.

The theoretician's lack of reserve, if one may still speak by today's standards, is shocking to the modern reader, but so also is his lack of logic: this is witnessed in his citing foremost what he insists to be taboo. Of importance is the fact that the novelist's most refined laughers do not hesitate to laugh at Panurge's equally "refined" flatulence. Both Joubert and Rabelais offer comment and illustration on the link between fear and sudden unintentional excretion. When Rabelais's *gros enflé de Conseillier* substantiates Joubert's category of the comic fall, he shows also that the theorist is literally earthier in his tastes than will be his *confrère* of the nineteenth century (Bergson). Rabelais improves upon Joubert's idea of the comic fall by nuancing it with the symbolic *cheute* of the Parisian gentlewoman. Another difference between Renaissance and today is the apparent lack of concern (by our standards) for an individual's personal comfort or welfare. Slapstick is much more heartily appreciated not only by Rabelais's laughers but by sixteenth-century man in general, if we are to trust Joubert's examples on this point. The logical tightness of the treatise is impaired at times, but this "fault" is often counterbalanced by striking illustrations that reveal or typify Renaissance thought: antithesis and oxymoron are fundamental figures in both doctors' style. Perhaps of utmost interest and importance for the modern reader is the fact that the group's lust for laughter seems far more tyrannical and far less concerned about the personal feelings of the individual singled out as a laughingstock. Yet at the same time—offering thus a sort of paradox—an exuberant charity seems to be engendered by this rough mirth, mirth that we might find too antisocial. It is a hilarity that is often scatological, often anti-Bergsonian in its emphasis on the physiological, and, in its pain-pleasure mixture, almost always ambiguous.

Chapter 3

Purpose and Elaboration

BESIDES THOSE LAUGHABLE deeds that hinge upon chance are those that are directed by conscious will. Acts done purposely that cause laughter, "sciammant, & de pansee expresse" ("with full consciousness, and on purpose" [*TR*, 20–21]), complete the *laughable in deed*. Joubert lists only two subdivisions under laughable deeds consciously executed: imitation and practical jokes.

Imitation

The concept of *imitation* is, for Joubert, essentially a matter of pretending to be the opposite of what one is. It is clearly explained in his three examples, all based upon antithesis: an old man acting like a child ("vn vieilhard se iouë par les ruës an maniere d'anfat"), a well-known and very respected person donning a strange costume ("quelqu'vn, autremant fort notable & d'apparance . . . se deguise an etrange fasson"), and finally, a fool pretending to be a wise man by taking on his manner of dressing, of making gestures, and of speech ("vn fou contrefait le sage, d'habit, de gestes, & de parolle"). All this claims Joubert, is cause for laughter: *tout cela nous fait rire.* The reason, of course, is that these cases correspond to Joubert's general theory discussed earlier: there is ugliness, but no sympathy, "pour ne conuenir aus personnes & etre laid, & de ce qu'il n'y ha point de mal, qui merite cōpassion" (*TR,* 21).

Bergson defines *imitation* as the ability to bring out the element of automatism one has allowed to creep into one's self: "Imiter quelqu'un, c'est dégager la part d'automatisme qu'il a laissé s'introduire dans sa personne."[1] It is interesting to note that the mental traits common to the nineteenth century (mass mechanization espoused by the industrial revolution) seep into Bergson's concept of imitation just as sixteenth-century thought inspires Joubert's idea of imitation (antithesis and contraries).[2]

There are, in the comic novel, two episodes that must be recalled constantly because of their humorous richness. We have seen one of these scenes only briefly, but the other has already been partially analyzed above. The subdivision under discussion helps bring out still more of the mirthful virtues of Panurge and the sneezing ladies. Although the incident involves neither a *vieilhard,* nor a dignitary, nor a fool, as in Joubert's example, it does present an antithesis in the person of Panurge imitating and mocking a *dame raffinée* in speech and in manner: " 'Et cest ouvrage, est il de Flandres, ou de Haynault?' Et puis tiroit son mouchenez, disant: 'Tenez, tenez, voyez en cy de l'ouvrage; elle est de Foutignan ou de Foutarabie' " (" 'Now is this Flemish work or from Hainault?' Next he would pull out his handkerchief and say: 'Look, just look at this. Here's fine work for you. It's from Spunkignan or Spunkarabia' ").[3] This particular episode, because of its simultaneous participation in several comic categories, might be most successfully analyzed by passing it through Joubert's complete comic grid. Although the actual laughter of the ladies justifies the category under discussion (imitation), it is obvious that some of the theorist's other categories illumine to a fuller extent the comic value of a given situation or even, eventually, of an entire comic work. They accomplish this by calling to mind the multiple aspects present that contribute to laughter. Here, for example, Rabelais's characters show that the possibility of laughter is not remote when a puck such as Panurge imitates gentlewomanly ways. But Panurge's imitation does not limit itself to the ladies' appearance. He also takes it upon himself to give an upside-down-world image of their very laughter-infested sternutation:

Ce pendent il petoit comme un roussin, et les femmes ryoient luy disans:
"Comment, vous petez, Panurge?
— Non foys, disoit il, madame; mais je accorde au contrepoint de la musique que vous sonnez du nez."

All the time he would fart like a horse, and they would say with a laugh! "How you do fart, Panurge." "Oh dear, no, Madam," he would reply, "I'm merely tuning myself to the counterpoint of the music you are making with your nose."

Paradoxically, then, Panurge's imitation is refinedly gross; such a situation in oxymoron recalls vividly Joubert's formula for laughter.

The other episode, also dealing with Panurge, concerns less the speech and gestures and more the manner of dressing. When the trickster seeks advice from Epistemon on the subject of marriage, the latter points out to Panurge that, because of his *desguisement,* everyone was making fun of him: "toute la voix publicque estoit consommée en mocqueries." Both of these cases bring about laughter in the novel, each confirming at least partially Joubert's subdivision. Only partial substantiation may be affirmed thus far, however, since both occasions draw their laughter from other categories as well.

But other aspects of imitation in connection with hilarity are to be seen in Rabelais that solidify the theorist's construct of mimesis. During the prologue to *Gargantua,* the narrator speaks about *silenes:*

Silenes estoient jadis petites boites, telles que voyons de present es bouticques des apothecaires, pinctes au dessus de figures joyeuses et frivoles, comme de harpies, satyres, oysons bridez, lievres cornuz, canes bastées, boucqs volans, cerfz limonniers et aultres telles pinctures contrefaictes à plaisir pour exciter le monde à rire. . . .

Sileni, in days gone by, were little boxes, like the ones we now see in apothecaries' shops with joyful and frivolous figures painted on them, such as harpies, satyrs, trussed birds, horned hares, saddled ducks, flying goats, harnessed deer, and other pictures of the same kind designed expressly to incite people to laugh. . . .[4]

Here is a case where two levels of imitation are developed, one concrete, the other abstract. On the literal level, some unknown agent has painted the apothecary cans to make them look as if they contained something other than they really do. This recalls Joubert's basic antithetical imitation motif of being-appearance. The purpose for which such *contrefaçon* is perpetrated ("to incite people to laugh") may not be construed as the effect (actual laughter in the novel); nevertheless, the instance does harmonize with Joubert's conception of laughter. Mirth explodes into being when some ugliness and a mood of lightness are present. The figures on the *silenes* are most certainly grotesque, *contrefaictes à plaisir,* and their ugliness may not be said to arouse strong emotion since the narrator—still Alcofribas at this point—states that laughter is the purpose of this mascarading of apothecary boxes.

A figurative imitation parallels the *silenes* and uses them. Rabelais's work itself will imitate the nature of these boxes. It will not look as if it contains what it does. Thus far the mimetic enterprise is not complete, at least according to the sixteenth-century concept of imitation, for the imitation is not paradoxical. Interestingly enough, however, Rabelais's disavowal of the proposed silenes-book project, "si le croyez, vous n'approchez ne de pieds ne de mains à mon opinion" ("If you believe it, you do not come within a hand or a foot of my opinion"), ultimately recasts the work into the paradoxical state of appearing to be what it is not. Rabelais's work is not simple, it is paradoxical.[5] Making it imitate, momentarily, works such as *Fessepinte, La Dignité des Braguettes,* when its true nature is quite the opposite, is nothing short of laughable with respect to Joubert's concept of antithetical imitation.

Also connected with the foregoing example is the anecdote of Zeuxis the ancient portraitist cited in the *Quart Livre* by Pantagruel. The giant calls to mind several cases of men who met with a strange death. Zeuxis's fate was to die laughing at a painting he made of an old lady: " 'Zeuxis le painctre . . . subitement mourut à force de rire, considerant le minoys et portraict d'une vieille par luy representée en paincture. . . .'" ("Zeuxis, the painter . . . suddenly died of laughing as he looked at the features of an old hag in a portrait that he had painted").[6] Curious to say, Joubert discusses this precise death in the third book of his treatise. Both doctors doubtlessly drew from the same source: Erasmus. Joubert cites as reason for the artist's laughter the face that the old lady was making in the portrait: "Zeuxis . . . mourut an riant sans fin, de la grimace d'vne vielhe que luy maemes avoit peind" (*TR*, 347). If we are able to trust Joubert's reason for the artist's laughter, it is far from bold to assert that the unbridled mirth was due to a grotesque quality in the portrait.[7]

Two difficulties arise with this reference to laughter. First, it is a strange case and even Joubert admits that it is rare. Second, and more importantly, one may not give to this reference the same weight the other actual-life situations in the novel have by comparison. This is because Zeuxis is once-removed as a Rabelaisian character. Yet from another point of view, the fact of his presence is real. The novelist, in choosing the anecdote, makes the portraitist a character. It is above all the *quality* of his presence that pleads for his inclusion in the discussion: he is a martyr to laughter.

Despite the fact, then, that no real agent mimics reality in this case, imitation is the basis of a portrait. The artist passes on his powers of mimesis to the artifact. If Zeuxis made the portrait grimace, which is a face that is *contrefaicte*, one may say that Rabelais's use of the anecdote substantiates Joubert's category of imitation.

Pastoral Mockery

Far less difficult to discuss is the episode of the shepherds and the cakemakers. The mimesis takes place after the altercation and subsequent violence witnessed between Grandgousier's *bergiers* and the *fouaciers de Lerné*. The former, as they feast and laugh joyfully, mock the latter for their grumpiness and arrogance:

> Ce faict, et bergiers et bergieres feirent chere lye avecques ces fouaces et beaulx raisins, et se rigollerent ensemble au son de la belle bouzine, se mocquans de ces beaulx fouaciers glorieux, qui avoient trouvé male encontre. . . .

> When they were gone, the shepherds and shepherdesses feasted on their cakes and fine grapes, danced to the sound of pipes, and laughed at those proud bakers who had the worst of it. . . .[8]

We must assume that the shepherds and shepherdesses imitated playfully with appropriate gestures and speech the nasty disposition of their enemy. In fact, one might wonder in what other activity they could possibly be engaged, given the clause *se mocquans de ces beaulx fouaciers glorieux*. The

cakes and plump grapes, along with the sound of the bagpipes, are successful in calming the stirred emotions after the brief encounter between the
cakemakers and the shepherds. The glee outweighs the unhappiness, and
we recall that this proportion of the two emotions is critical according to
Joubert. Both the joy of the feast and the mocking of the enemy release the
laughter here, while the *belle bouzine,* as N. C. Carpenter suggests, "sets a
note of joyous rusticity."[9]

Joubert's concept of imitation is the fruit of sixteenth-century thought.
Traits of this same thought are often expressed in mirthful passages where
Rabelais unfolds diverse forms of this particular concept. On a more general
scale, Alfred Glauser notes in Rabelais this poetic tendency toward self-
contradiction that characterizes the theorist's notion of imitation:

> Il sera un immense poète en contrebande; il chante, mais il prétendra par
> pudeur que sa voix est un cri, le propos d'un ivrogne. Si sa voix tend vers la
> douceur, il veut la rendre rauque; tenté par le lyrisme, il fera tout pour lui
> échapper.

> He will be an immense unofficial poet; he sings but will claim out of shame
> that his voice is a screeching, the words of a drunkard. If his voice leans
> toward sweetness, he wants to make it raucous; tempted by lyricism, he will
> do everything to escape it.[10]

As is the case with Joubert's conception of the act of laughter, so, too, on
the level of this particular category of the laughable, two contrary entities
come to inhabit one person, expression, or concept. This is the substratum
of Rabelais's mimetic expression and Joubert's theory. Alcofribas's disavowal, since it obeys the laws of comic imitation of the time, may be
understood for what it is: an attempt on the author's part at Renaissance
hilarity, a sort of exercise in mental and physiological oxymoron.

Practical Jokes

The second and last subdivision under deeds purposefully executed has
the title *practical jokes,* "tours q̄ nous faisons pour nous mocquer ou andōm-

ager autruy" ("tricks we do to laugh or to hurt another" [*TR*, 22]). Three examples of practical jokes elucidate this grouping of laughable deeds: undoing a person's clothing ("comme si à vn qui n'y panse pas, on decout sa robe"), water throwing ("si nous jettons d'eau sus vn qui ne s'an auise pas"), and setting someone to the task of looking for something that we ourselves have hidden ("si nous mettons vn autre an peine de chercher quelque chose de petite importāce, laquelle nous auons cachée"). These, according to Joubert, are only a few of such numberless little tricks, "sāblables infinies bourdes," all causing laughter. The only provision is that they be pulled in fun, and that no real damage or suffering be inflicted, even though such might seem to be the case: "qu'il n'y ha point de vray outrage, deplaisir, ou dommage, combien que l'apparance y soit" (*TR*, 22–23).

This last sentence requires a moment of reflection. It is pertinent to recall Joubert's—and Aristotle's—general theory on laughter, in particular that part dealing with *ugliness* and *lack of pity*. Obviously such terms are relative. We remember that concepts such as *dommage* have changed over time, as was seen in Joubert's Chaucerian example of the red-hot iron. What constitutes *vray outrage, deplaisir, ou dommage* is less remotely connected to death than we are prepared to admit today. Belonging to a century and a society in which physical or mental anomalies are either kept from the public or committed to institutions, we must make an effort to adjust our minds accordingly in reading texts of the sixteenth century. Plagues, scattering corpses, and cries of pain throughout town and countryside recurred frequently.[11] The phrase *combien que l'apparance y soit* emphasizes the notion of gravity as a desirable aspect in the *tour*. Although we may not claim that such apparent seriousness is a necessary condition to the Renaissance prank, a strong dose of severity is an expressed preference on the part of the theorist.

Stripping and Striping or Nakedness and Cruelty

Practical jokes can hardly be mentioned in the same breath as Rabelais without Panurge coming to mind. He is the *farceur* of the comic novelist's creation.[12] One may say without reserve that he always has more than one trick up his sleeve (*plus d'un tour dans son sac*). Chapter XVI of *Pantagruel* is made up of a series of the prankster's mischievous delights, two of which anticipate the theoretician's first example of denudation. One of the pock-

ets of Panurge's bag of tricks is stuffed with little hooks and clasps destined to bring about an automatic involuntary striptease:

> ... force provisions de haims et claveaulx, dont il acouploit souvent les
> hommes et les femmes en compagnies où ilz estoient serrez, et mesmement
> celles qui portoyent robbes de tafetas armoisy, et, à l'heure qu'elles se vou-
> loyent departir, elles rompoyent toutes leurs robbes. . . .

> ... a large supply of hooks and buckles, with which he would fasten men
> and women together, in places where they were crowded close. And he
> especially chose those who were wearing thin taffeta gowns, so that when
> they tried to get apart they tore all their clothes. . . .[13]

A major difference, of course, is that Panurge makes his victims the effi-
cient cause of their own undoing. Another means proves to be equally
effective and even more amusing in spite of the discomfort that it engenders:

> Item, il y avoit une autre poche pleine de alun de plume, dont il gettoit
> dedans le doz des femmes qu'il voyoit les plus acrestées, et les faisoit des-
> pouiller devant tout le monde. . . .

> Item, he had another pocket full of itching powder, which he threw down
> the backs of those women whom he saw carrying their heads the highest, and
> so made them strip before all the world. . . .

These scenes from Rabelais obviously make Joubert's slot of *tours* more
trustworthy for use elsewhere in Rabelais as well as in other sixteenth-
century French literature. But they do more; besides confirming indirectly
still another of Joubert's categories, *les parties hôteuses*, they indicate also, by
virtue of their closeness to the theorist's examples, contemporary comic
commonplaces.[14]

These scenes could also be seen as exemplifying the symbolic *chute ·
comique*. Similarly, the very example cited to illustrate the literal comic fall,
the bloated counselor in the mire, also corroborates the present category of
playful pranks. The important difference is that in the foregoing chapter,
the laughter of the victims or the observers was the determining factor.

Even Panurge's laughter entered into the analysis, but only insofar as he was an onlooker. Here, however, it is the mirthful Panurge as efficacious physician of the comic organism who justifies rementioning the episode and analyzing it from this point of view. For memory's sake, we recall the scene briefly:

> Quand le gros enflé de Conseillier, ou autre, a prins son bransle pour monter sus, ilz tombent tous platz comme porcz devant tout le monde, et aprestent à rire pour plus de cent francs. Mais je me rys encores davantage, c'est que, eulx arrivez au logis, ilz font fouetter monsier de paige comme seigle vert.

> Then when some bloated counselor or other has taken his swing to get up, he'll fall flat as a hog before everybody, and provide more than a hundred francs' worth of laughter. But I have a bigger laugh still, because when they get back home they have Master Page beaten like green rye.[15]

Panurge gladly supports the financial burden of providing a banquet for the pages. He finds the reward well worth the cost: " 'Par ainsi, je ne me plains point ce que m'a cousté à les bancqueter' " (" 'So I don't complain of what it cost me to banquet them' "). Alcofribas makes it a point to suggest that Panurge's two hundred fourteen ways of spending money are mostly given to procuring laughter for himself and others. In this sense, it is Panurge rather than the narrator who has the role of *architriclin,* master of ceremonies, in the Rabelaisian feast of mirth, ordinating the comic events of the novel and assuring their powers of engendering hilarity, as well as providing much personal satisfaction: "mais je me rys encore dadvantage."

The distinction established between Panurge the observer and Panurge the perpetrator of comic deeds necessitates reviewing the technical aspects of the *tour à la dame Parisianne.* Here he is seen in terms of his authorship of the comic enterprise:

> Le jour de la vigile, Panurge chercha tant d'un cousté et d'aultre qu'il trouva une lycisque orgoose, laquelle il lya avecques sa ceinture et la mena en sa chambre, et la nourrist très bien ce dict jour et toute la nuyct. Au matin la tua et en print ce que sçavent les geomantiens Gregoys, et le mist en pieces le plus menu qu'il peut, et les emporta bien cachées et alla où la dame devoit aller pour suyvre la procession. . . .

Et . . . promptement sema la drogue qu'il avoit sur elle en divers lieux, et mesmement au replis de ses manches et de sa robbe. . . .

On the vigil of that day, Panurge hunted in all directions for a hot sheep-dog bitch; and when he had secured her with his belt, he took her to his room and fed her very well on that day and all the next night. In the morning he killed her and removed that part which the Greek necromancers know. This he cut into the smallest possible pieces, which he took away well wrapped up. Then he went to the church where the lady must go to follow the procession. . . .

And . . . deftly sprinkled the drug that he was carrying on to various parts of her, chiefly on the pleats of her sleeves and her dress. . . .[16]

His laughter is one of intentionality more than of surprise. One can easily liken the long-suffering smile of the prankster to a vigil light that finally turns incendiary as the whittlings of the comic's patient labors accumulate: *Et Panurge de rire* ("And Panurge laughed"). Pantagruel and the lady's chambermaids laugh in their astonishment: they saw only the result. Panurge, on the other hand, lives the irreversible mechanisms. He arranges their intricate parts; they can only lend this same complexity to his laughter, and Panurge then reaps the fruits of what he had so diligently sown.

Just as Joubert theorizes that laughter, physiologically speaking, is not a simple matter of *liesse,* but a mingling of contrary emotions, so, too, Rabelais bears witness to an ambivalent quality in Renaissance mirth. The counselor tumbles, the lady is led to the pillar of ridicule, the page is whipped, all to Panurge's delight. All the victims are stripped and scourged, some figuratively, others literally, while Panurge, Rabelais's flagellator, laughs.

Frère Jan's Explosive Trick

Although Panurge is by far the prankster par excellence in the novel, Frère Jan is also capable of a nasty trick. An example is the last practical joke of the *Quart Livre.* A final blast of laughter accompanies the discharge of the *basilic* in the final chapter of the four authentic books of Rabelais. Frère Jan is the instigator of this *grande finale.* Panurge's inordinate fear pushes the monk to dream up a means of giving him the scare of his life. After much talk about devils, Panurge goes below to hide while Frère Jan, Pantagruel, Epistemon, and the rest of the merry band remain on deck.

The time is propitious for a light conspiracy involving heavy pieces:

> "— Escouttez doncques, dist frere Jan, ce pendant que les chormes y font aiguade. Panurge là bas contrefaict le loup en paille. Voulez vous bien rire? Faictes mettre le feu en ce basilic que voyez près le chasteau guaillard."

> "Listen then," said friar John. "While the crews are fetching water, Panurge is as snug as a bug below. Would you have a good laugh? Now see this basilisk beside the fo'c'stle. Let's have it fired. . . ."[17]

Pantagruel finds the idea to his liking. He orders the master artilleryman to set off the huge cannon. Upon hearing the deafening roar of Pantagruel's *basilic,* the other cannonmasters of the fleet touch off their heavy pieces: "Croyez qu'il y eut beau tintamarre" ("There was a fine din, take my word for it"). Panurge, convinced that hell's foundations were trumpeting skyward, reacts physiologically along the lines that fear commands, as already discussed in the previous chapter. Needless to say, the nautical stratagem caused no small amount of mirth among the tricksters. It is as though Rabelais, in this last episode that closes the authentic novel, feels compelled to chastize once and for all Panurge's previous comic wrath. If any misgivings linger with regard to the puck's behavior—or even his lack of compassion in outsmarting Dindenault, which we discuss next—all slates are even in this final scene of poetic justice where even the outwitter is outwitted. All share in the laughter here: prankster, victim, and onlookers are united in a common *sursum corda* before the besmirched Panurge who, not to be outdone, bursts out laughing last and best over his own Rabelaisian undoing.

Dindenault's Death and the Drowning Parisians

Perhaps the most devilish trick that Panurge devises is that which constitutes the Dindenault episode, covered by chapters VI through VIII of the *Quart Livre.* The sheep merchant pays with his life the antagonizing and the greed that he manifests in his dealings with Panurge. All important to an understanding of the scene is Panurge's invitation to Epistemon and Frère Jan to participate, albeit passively, in the pleasure of outfoxing the fox. They will follow him as he goes about setting the trap:

Panurge dist secretement à Epistemon et à frere Jan: "Retirez vous icy un peu
à l'écart, et joyeusement passez temps à ce que voirez. Il y aura bien beau jeu,
si la chorde ne rompt."

Panurge whispered to Epistemon and Friar John: "Just go a little way off,
and you'll be very tickled by what you'll see. There's going to be a high old
game, if the rope doesn't break."[18]

The expression *si la chorde ne rompt* is an allusion to the ropes and pulleys
and various other mechanical contraptions, all of which supported the
awesome and terrible events, the stage effects, of the medieval mystery
plays.[19] In this context, it is the ordonnance of the comic mechanism.

The episode matches Joubert's definition of the category under discussion: tricks we play *pour nous moquer ou andomager autruy*. But the modern
reader may conceivably question any similarity beyond this point in view of
the qualifying clause added by the theorist: "but only in unimportant
things, and in fun." It is necessary to investigate how Dindenault's loss of
life and fortune can fade into insignificance and be viewed with laughing
eyes. These are matters with which the comic author deals creatively. Since
the laws formulated, or rather revealed, by the theoretician rely on laughter
as it is caused or as it is recorded by the author of the comic deed, the
problem must be approached from the perpetrator's point of view. But the
question then becomes who is the perpetrator? Panurge? Rabelais? Epistemon and Frère Jan? Sixteenth-century readers? Finally, today's reader? Do
we not, all of us, participate in the comic deed?

As we have already seen, the entire episode is built upon an important
premise: that of providing pleasure ("Retirez vous icy un peu à l'escart, et
joyeusement passez temps à ce que voirez"), says Panurge. The purpose is
clear from the instigator's point of view, as it is from the theorist's: it is for
fun, *an jeu* (*TR*, 22). But can one make the simple step from paucity of
matter ("chose qui n'importe") to Dindenault's tragic fall merely by
reiterating the a priori all-is-in-fun?[20] For the comic novelist it is only a
beginning, even if it is a foundation. Two entire chapters are spent doing
an essential task: they reduce in various ways the serious matter. They
prepare and justify both the laughter and the "tragedy" to come. In this
sense, Rabelais shows us by such elaboration that it is not a simple matter,
but the question remains how precisely is it funny? To label the comic
problem of the Dindenault episode a false one created by the modern reader

is tempting but needs some defense. Besides this, as we shall see in reviewing the episode in the light of Joubert, other textual factors are involved.

Both Panurge, actual perpetrator of the comic deed, and the sixteenth-century observers in the novel, namely Epistemon and Frère Jan, along with the captain and crew—all passive collaborators with Panurge—take pleasure in the destruction of Dindenault. Today's reader, if he agrees at all that one is able to enjoy this outcome, emphasizes that this is true only after a considerable period during which the merchant is presented as a detestable character. Not only is he despicable for what he is, an arrogant *bourgeois* whose ability to exasperate is unprecedented, but also, as Robert Marichal points out, for what he represents: ignorance.[21] Ignorance is the unpardonable sin if we are to judge from the magnitude of the chastisement that the word-spouting merchant is about to receive.[22] He is a sort of *autodidacte avant la lettre,* but to make matters worse, he has not even the merit of being well intentioned as was the Sartrian character. While all these charges approach a figurative critical mass, a final capital fault is introduced that aggravates his case to the point of detonation: Dindenault is also guilty of being a bad humorist. What more irreparable breach could exist in a world whose values are comic? The merchant tries not only Panurge's patience, but the other crew members' as well. All must listen to his seemingly interminable attempts at cleverness. At length, his pointless ramblings become unbearable:

"— Patience, respondit Panurge. Mais expedions.

— Et quand, dist le marchant, vous auray je, nostre amy, mon voisin, dignement loué les membres internes? L'espaule, les esclanges, les gigotz, le hault cousté, la poitrine, le faye, la ratelle, les trippes, la guogue, la vessye, dont on joue à la balle; les coustelettes, dont on faict en Pygmion les beaulx petits arcs pour tirer noyaulx de cerises contre les grues; la teste, dont, avecques un peu de soulphre, on fait une mirificque decoction pour faire viander les chiens constippez du ventre?

— Bren, bren, dist le patron de la nauf au marchant, c'est trop icy barguigné. Vends luy si tu veux; si tu ne veulx, ne l'amuse plus."

"Patience," said Panurge. "But let's get on."

"How can I ever tell you the true merits of the internal organs, my dear friend and neighbor?" asked the dealer. "The shoulders, the haunches, the legs, the neck, the breast, the liver, the spleen, the tripes, the paunch, and the bladder, which they play ball with, and the ribs which they use in Pygmy-land for making little bows to shoot cherry-stones at the cranes, and the head, to which they add a little sulphur to make a marvellous decoction for loosening the bowels of constipated dogs."

"Piss and shit," said the ship's captain to the dealer. "There's far too much haggling here. Sell it to him if you're going to. But if you don't want to, stop playing the fool with him."[23]

Even the captain, speaking for all those suffering the din of the blabbering braggart, has had enough of Dindenault's dim sparks of wit. Joubert condemns in these words such a lack of gracefulness in exercising the art of humor:

> Le plaisir & bōne grace se perd, quad ils ne vienet à propos, an tãs & lieu: ou ils sont tãt reiterés, qu'on s'an ennuie.

> The pleasure and gracefulness are lost when pleasantries do not come at the right time and place, or when they are so often repeated that they are boring. (TR, 35)

Thus sixteenth-century comic theory as well as Rabelais's practice take dead aim at Dindenault. Panurge performs the chastisement, at which point the episode draws quickly to a close. In an awesome scene reminiscent of divine vengeance calling upon the earth to swallow up entire nations guilty of heinous crimes, Dindenault and his muttony mammon are engulfed in the maws of the deep.

Strictly speaking, the episode corresponds inversely to the theorist's illustration since the victims are carried into the water rather than undergoing a mere soaking. On the moral plane, however, the correlation is much tighter due to the element of surprise. It animates both the theory ("si nous iettons d'eau sus vn qui ne s'an auise pas") and the heart of Rabelais's (Panurge's) successful *ruse:*

> Soubdain, je ne sçay comment, le cas feut subit, je ne eu loisir le considerer, Panurge, sans aultre chose dire, jette en pleine mer son mouton criant et bellant.

All at once—I don't know how; things happened so swiftly that I hadn't time to watch them—Panurge without another word threw his crying and bleating sheep into the sea.[24]

Joubert considers speed an almost indispensable factor in a marginal note: "La vitesse et comme la sauce, qui dõne l'appetit de rire" ("Speed is like the sauce which gives the appetite to laugh" [TR, 35]).

Curiously enough, it is the tragedy's closing commentary that offers the proof of its laugh-engendering virtue, but at the same time raises the modern reader's misgivings with regard to the humor of the episode. Panurge asks Frère Jan his reaction to the affair. The monk's enjoyment of the scene, although certain, does not go without at least one reservation— but not in the expected sense. He seems every bit as cruel by today's reader's standards as Panurge when he remarks that the money for the sheep would not have been lost had payment been withheld until sending them all off to sea. Panurge, as was the case with the whipped page, gladly pays the fee of laughter, but it is this blatant lack of pity and this excessive parsimony on the part of Frère Jan that dismay and even alienate some of today's readers. Screech and Calder speak of this very difficulty.[25]

Still one may see in this lack of sympathy two avenues of interpretation: one taken by the Renaissance reader, the other by the modern reader. The former interprets it as an invitation to mirth due to its inappropriateness, as Joubert suggests: "malseant & peu conuenable" ("inappropriate and unfitting"). The latter is tempted to search for a deeper meaning either beyond the comic or within the comic: beyond the comic because he finds Dindenault's death unwarrantable and the reaction to it too flippant; within the comic, but generically, because, still fundamentally uncomfortable about Dindenault's sort, it must be treated as unreality. The latter is the solution de facilité; the outcome will always be funny because we are dealing with a comic novel. Although eminently sound, it is still not entirely satisfying.

Joubert's theory is able to offer other alternatives. A possible answer to the problem of Frère Jan's harsh reply lies in the assumption that he is doing a parody of the merchant's avariciousness, which has just cost him such a terrible price. Such mimicry on the part of the monk corresponds already to Joubert's category of imitation: Frère Jan is many things in the novel, but he is never miserly. Such contrary behavior, by sixteenth-century standards, is laughable.

Before bringing the whole of Joubert's theory to bear upon the Dindenault incident, we must examine the laugher's reactions and actions as Rabelais portrays them. Panurge, who thoroughly enjoys the prank, "'Vertus Dieu, j'ay eu du passetemps pour plus de cinquante mille francs'" ("'I had some shitten good fun for my money!'"... "Why, that joke was worth more than fifty thousand francs'"), reveals the essence of his own ethical system according to which he himself metes out pleasure for good turns, and for ill turns, pain or punishment:

"Jamais homme ne me feist plaisir sans recompense, ou recongnoissance pour le moins. Je ne suys point ingrat et ne le feuz, ne seray. Jamais homme ne me feist desplaisir sans repentence, ou en ce monde, ou en l'autre."

"No man ever did me a good turn without getting a reward, or at least an acknowledgement. I'm not an ungrateful man, I never was, and never will be. And nobody's ever done me a bad turn without being sorry for it, either in this world or the next."[26]

The application of Panurge's system to the Dindenault episode brings out sharply the two sides of the issue: Panurge is a good humorist, and the laughers are with him; but Dindenault does not succeed in amusing the crew—on the contrary. Two tricksters are vying, and the observers must identify with the clever humorist from the very beginning according to the invitation of Panurge: "'Retirez vous icy un peu à l'escart, et joyeusement passez temps.'" Allowing pity to gain a foothold would constitute a breach in faith; it is to be interpreted as a commitment to the side of the clumsy jokester. It is a road that leads to gravity and compassion, not to laughter. Rabelais does not reward such ill faith; one has only to observe those who commit such comic apostasy.

But a new textual factor puts another twist in the problem at this point. Panurge's pleasure-pain principle will only hold true for the modern reader in the 1548 edition. With the publication of the entire *Quart Livre* in 1552, one witnesses an additional commentary made by Frère Jan.[27] The monk condemns Panurge for appointing himself as an agent of justice:

"— Tu, dist frere Jan, te damne comme un vieil diable. Il est escript: *Mihi vindictam, et caetera.* Matiere de breviaire."

"You're damning yourself like an old devil," answered Friar John. "It is written: *mihi vindictam,* etc.—Vengeance is mine. It's breviary stuff, that is."

The upshot of this addition in terms of our discussion is significant. Whether the monk's remark is interpreted by Panurge (or by readers of any century) as a supplemental piece of scriptural satire,[28] or a serious accusation of Panurge's merciless and heavy-handed justice, enters the question only secondarily here. By evoking at this precise moment the concept of justice and retribution, Panurge's ethical system and Dindenault's death are, of necessity, resummoned to mind for a second scrutinizing. The problem then becomes the color this reevaluation assumed in the Renaissance mind as opposed to the color it acquires in the modern mind.

What might have been construed as simple comic retribution in 1548 is made expressly ambiguous by Rabelais in 1552. The opposition riding the confrontation of Panurge's pleasure-pain system and the Christian framework based upon a merciful but just almighty agent is apparent. Also apparent is the fact that no choice is made: the case hangs eternally, both sides presented, neither approved or condemned. Ambiguity reigns triumphant. All important, however, is *how* this ambiguity is read.

Robert Marichal sees the problem clearly for the modern reader as he sums up *l'humour rabelaisien* in Dindenault's undoing: one simply does not know what to make of it. All footholds are unstable.[29] Rabelaisian treachery seems a more fitting term for Marichal's appreciation of the novelist's humor. Mistrust gives way to actual terror in some more recent critics with respect to Rabelais's toying with language and logic.[30] Ambivalence in emotional experiences and ambiguity in thought and in speech dismay twentieth-century man. Yet Panurge's laughter, shared by his friends, corresponds to Joubert's definition of the joke. The Renaissance observer or reader, far from seeing treachery or danger in consciously perpetrated ambiguity in such a context (*an jeu*), knew exactly what to make of Frère Jan's perplexing remark: matter for laughter.

Thus far, then, it has been possible to cope with the episode on Renaissance comic terms without recourse to the *in extremis* weapon of generic definition to defend the contemporary reaction to Dindenault's final passage. But we now have to deal with his death directly. Here two specialists as different in their approaches to Rabelais as M. A. Screech and Alfred Glauser unite in treating Rabelaisian death as unreality.[31] In an unreal world, death itself is unreal, therefore devoid of emotion and therefore ultimately laughable. Yet a final point stops us from subscribing to the all-is-in-fun: must the modern reader not agree that there is a considerable difference between his or her reaction to Dindenault's drowning and the similar fate of the Parisians in the Gargantuan urinary cataract? A brief comparison of these two death scenes will indicate whether annihilation of the problem is a viable solution in terms of sixteenth-century comic theory.

Gargantua decides to celebrate his coming to Paris by giving the Parisians much more than a token of his arrival. He commemorates the event by a baptism of fire in which they are to receive a new name. The christening clearly fits into Joubert's category of dirty tricks pulled in fun:

> "Je leur voys donner le vin, mais ce ne sera que par rys."
>
> Lors, en soubriant, destacha sa belle braguette, et tirant sa mentule en l'air, les compissa si aigremant qu'il en noya deux cens soixante mille quatre cens dix et huyt, sans les femmes et petiz enfans.
>
> Quelque nombre d'iceulx evada ce pissefort à legiereté de pieds, et, quand furent au plus hault de l'Université, suans, toussans, crachans et hors d'haleine, commencerent à renier et à jurer, les ungs en cholere, les aultres par rys: "Carymary, carymara! Par saincte Mamye, nous son baignez par ryz!" Dont fut depuis la ville nommée *Paris,* laquelle auparavant on appelloit Leucece. . . .

> "I'm going to give them wine—but only *par ris,* for fun, that is."
>
> When he finished speaking, smiling, he unfastened his fine codpiece, and drawing out his pleasure rod, he bepissed them so fiercely that he drowned two hundred sixty thousand, four hundred and eighteen of them, not counting women and children.
>
> Some escaped this mighty pissflood by fleetness of foot. And when they reached the highest point of the University, sweating, coughing, spitting, and breathless, they began to curse and swear, some in anger, others for fun: "Carymary, carymara! By St. Mamie, we are drenched *par ris."* And from that day on the city was called Paris. It had been called Leucetia before then. . . .[32]

Although the number of victims ("deux cens soixante mille quatre cens dix et huyt" excluding women and children) in the mass drowning outstrips by far the population of Paris at the time, there are still a few who escape to carry on their freshly acquired epithet. This handful of survivors find themselves short of breath, but not to the point of being unable to express their emotion amidst the abominable deluge. Some of the Parisians—for such is their name now—explode in cosmopolitan blasphemy, especially in earlier editions.[33] Others, overwhelmed by the humor of it all, actually laugh upon seeing themselves the victims of such an enormous joke: ". . . les aultres par rys: 'Carymary, carymara!'"

In the *Quart Livre*, however, the closing note is decidedly more tragic for today's reader: there are no survivors, "tous furent en mer portez et noyez miserablement." The only emotion witnessed is fear: "Le marchant, tout effrayé de ce que davant ses yeux perir voyoit et noyer ses moutons, s'efforçoit les empescher et retenir tout de son pouvoir. Mais c'estoit en vain." ("The dealer, in his alarm at seeing his sheep perish by drowning, tried to prevent them and held them back with all his might. But it was useless."). The merchant's former loquacity is stopped. No sound is uttered as the sea swallows shepherds, sheep, and merchant in a watery silence. In the Gargantuan inundation the victims revolt—some with anger, some with laughter—in the face of what can only be called a revolting situation. Here the modern reader is able to cope with their death because it does not seem as real. The destruction is not total because there are survivors and even laughers. In the case of the utter destruction of Dindenault, however, the modern reader cannot laugh, because his death is seen as real. Indeed, in the brief hush, one seems to hear resonances of the Last Judgment, soon to be overtly alluded to in Frère Jan's *mihi vindictam*.

These two episodes are poles apart for today's reader. According to Joubert, however, and Rabelais, both episodes are clearly laughable. Even the monk's added reply, which enhances ambiguity, poses no problem whatever for the theoretician inasmuch as such ambivalence is the very fountainhead of Renaissance laughter. The problem in approaching the laughable in Rabelais is one of foregoing the ease with which we, as modern readers, make certain logical distinctions and of making the effort to practice others. In the Dindenault episode, for example, Rabelais spends several pages dramatizing an encounter, reducing the interest camps to two polar entities: the graceful and the maladroit. When he does this, he is in the process of building a comic system, the metaphysics so to speak, upon which Panurge's ethical framework and, ultimately, Joubert's theory depend. A modern reader would probably focus less in these chapters on taking for granted that one side is sly and the other clumsy than on the clever elaboration involved in actually depicting them as such. In other

words, the novelist's art for such a reader is the ability to make one believe
in this confrontation of the clever trickster and the boorish jokester; it is as
if this were the sole comic matter at hand. In this sense, up to a given
moment in this matching of wits, a portion of Rabelais's comic art is
possibly accepted, but probably overlooked by the modern mind, only to
be appreciated as, say, Rabelais's dramatic art.

This particular moment that changes all is, of course, Panurge's enjoyment in vanquishing his opponent. Here Rabelais steps beyond the bounds
set by the esthetic system of today's reader. What had been an off-stage
difficulty for the twentieth-century reader now becomes the central dilemma. Able to appreciate Rabelais's dramatic art in depicting the development of the scene, he now finds himself incapable of embracing his
comic art at the denouement. Yet just as the sixteenth-century reader was
fixed in his structures, esthetic and comic, refusing to see the Parisians
drown one way and Dindenault die in another, the modern reader, hyper-
sensitive by tradition and education, responds to the immediate reality so
vigorously brushed before him. The guarantee of levity for the Renaissance
laugher is in the aside to Epistemon and Frère Jan; no amount of reflection
on the episode will change his predisposition. The die is set at the beginning: the fact that harm is done to another (*andõmager autruy*) is less of a
concern than the fact that it is in fun (*an jeu*). Laughter ratifies the theoretician's category in spite of the modern reader's misgivings; what Rabelais
most probably wanted to do was to enhance the comic force of the episode
by adding the *mihi vindictam* in 1552. Once again, it seems that the
twentieth-century mind, intent upon seeing deeper (*la pensée profonde*), ends
up seeing only tragic depth where the novelist, in harmony with Joubert's
theory, was seeking a deceptive comic shallowness.

Summary

Imitation as Joubert conceives of it and as Rabelais frequently gives it
form in his novel is based upon antithesis and paradox.[34] This is evident in
simple character portrayal as in Panurge's imitation of the *bonnes dames* and
in complex metaphorical structures such as the *silenes,* used by the narrator
to represent his own literary creation. The category is corroborated by
laughter both in part and in entirety on several occasions.

As for *vilains tours,* a sort of devilish meanness drives many of the characters of the novel to perpetrate what today's reader might well consider excessive practical jokes. Dindenault, the *escholier Limosin*, Frère Estienne, and the Chiquanous are but a few of the Rabelaisian victims whose ends, although involving physical pain or death, spur mirth among the pranksters and witnesses of such comic deeds.

The laughter of the Renaissance seems confused or even hostile by today's standards as it resounds over the mingling of contrary emotions and frolics with thought and logic in willful ambiguities; it might even appear cruel since it embraces much more suffering on the part of the *hostia comica* than twentieth-century esthetics will bear. Jean-Marie Domenach's *Le Retour du tragique* is proof enough of the unacceptableness of the term *comic* for the *homo patiens* of our century. Nevertheless, it is this laughter that determines the formulation of a comic theory and characterizes the execution of Rabelaisian comic practice. Rather than being a passive observer and victim of surprise, the laugher, as character or as reader, performs an active role in what must now be called the comic enterprise, as opposed to what had previously been merely a passive function in comic happenings. But the laughable deed constitutes only one half of Joubert's Aristotelian construct of *matiere du Ris*. We must now investigate the *laughable in word*.

Chapter 4

ě

Narration and Laughter

WE HAVE SEEN that Joubert, following tradition, divides the laughable into two areas: what is perceived by the eyes (*la vue*), and what we come to know through our sense of hearing (*l'ouye*). The major heading *laughable in word*—laughter provoked particularly by what is heard—also has two subdivisions in the theoretician's mind. The difference is between laughter brought about by the words themselves and laughter resulting from what is told, or narrated. Bergson enounces this very idea in the following terms: "Mais il faut distinguer entre le comique que le langage exprime et celui que le langage crée" ("It is necessary to distinguish between the comic that language expresses, and that which language creates").[1] Joubert relates the difference to the distinction between the senses of sight and hearing: "l'ouye ressoit des ridicules propres à soy, & d'autres communs à la vuë" ("The sense of hearing receives laughable matter proper to itself, and matter pertaining to the sense of sight" [*TR*, 29]). The *laughable in deed*, usually associated with the sense of sight, must not, however, be confused with the second subdivision of the *laughable in word* ("*ridicules . . . communs à la vuë*") because of the visible character in which both share.

The unattentive mind quickly falls victim to this error since both categories cover comic situations. A precise feature of Joubert's comic theory in contradistinction to later theories is that it always keeps the laugher in sharp focus. Inasmuch as the laugher's senses of sight and hearing constitute not only the ultimate receiver of the laughable, but also that which permits an orderly examination of the subject, the laugher plays a more important and less abstract role than he would within the confines of a more modern theory. After Immanuel Kant, comic situations are analyzed more and more in terms of their characteristics than with respect to their ultimate purpose or effect.[2]

By virtue of Joubert's basic conception of the laughable (human emotions in conflict) as well as his method of imposing order on the subject (physiological categories such as sight and hearing), a special place is inherently reserved for narration.[3] Narration, as a category, vies with that of actual comic events. In a sense it comprehends real-life situations (*laughable in deed*) simply by recounting them for the inner eye: "nous an rions presque autant, que si on les faisoit deuant nous" ("We laugh at them almost as much as if we were actually witnessing them" [*TR*, 29–30]). Joubert repeats his conviction, this time with less reserve, considering narration to possess as much laugh-engendering power as existing comic situations:

> . . . ceus [propos ridicules] qu'on recite auoir eté fais & vus, qui durant la narration samblet etre deuant les yeus: dont il auiēt, qu'on n'an rid pas moins, que si on les voyoit.

> . . . those [laughable stories] which are cited as having been done and seen, which during their narration seem to be before our eyes, whence it is that they are not laughed at less than if they were seen.

Thus the *laughable in word* might conceivably include the *laughable in deed*, but does not do so in the theoretician's mind since it is conceptualized in physiological terms: sight and hearing. Here the subdivision of sight under *laughable in word* is tagged "narration."

Creative Reciprocation of Word and Deed

Laughter, as it is conceived of by Joubert, springs from a comic deed, actually seen or heard recounted, which arouses in the laugher simultaneous contrary emotions. In the category under discussion (narration), the comic deed, perceived aurally by the eventual laugher, is of course recreated visually in his imagination as it is being told to him. This comic deed is known only, however, because it is being recreated verbally by a narrator. Although the narration is of necessity subsequent to the comic occurrence that it is seeking to revitalize, it is at the same time capable of liberating the deed from the past despite the expiration of its course of existence in reality. In thus freeing the comic deed from oblivion, comic narration has the virtue of being a continual recreation of the laughable. In this respect, humorous narration appears as the interphase between the laughable and laughter; it is at this point that comic history becomes comic art. Without the verbal testimony of the laugher (narration), the laughable remains the secret of the past. The laugher becomes narrator in recreating, in making present once again, the components of the comic deed. Thus the narrator bears witness to the comic deed through his narration of it, but only because he first bore witness to its comic virtues with his own laughter.

An example of such an occurrence is in chapter XL of the *Tiers Livre*. Bridoye the judge is expounding at length on the reasons for which he went through the trouble of examining the suits he knew he would eventually decide by a throw of the dice. In the web of legal and classical citations justifying the second reason (which was the physical exercise that poring over a lawsuit afforded his Honor), Bridoye recalls stepping in on a particular trial during which all present were playing tag. As the judge reminisces, the scene comes back to life and with the memory comes the laughter. The laugher is a certain Tielman Picquet whose mirth could be assigned to Joubert's category of *legers domages* discussed previously since it was occasioned by the playful smashing of legal birettas.[4] The important point here is the fact that Bridoye's narration calls forth the comic deed from the past, making laughter live once again.

Narrative Networks of Laughter

Narration convoys laughter in several instances under Rabelais's pen. In some cases the narration embraces and absorbs the reader literally. It transforms him into a character, a character that laughs at this narration that has just circumscribed him. In chapter XXXVIII of the *Quart Livre*, for exam-

ple, the author has the reader laugh at such supposedly serious and englob-
ing narration:

> Vous truphez ici, beuveurs, et ne croyez que ainsi soit en verité comme je
> vous raconte. Je ne sçaurois que vous en faire. Croyez le, si voulez; si ne
> voulez, allez y veoir. Mais je sçay bien ce que je veidz.
>
> Now you are laughing at me, my jolly boozers. You do not believe what I
> tell you is really true. I don't know what to do about you. Believe me if you
> like; and if you don't, go and see for yourselves. I know well enough what I
> saw.[5]

Rabelais confirms his choice of the laughing reader, or at least his preference for such a reader, at the end of the chapter, once again admonishing
him for his laughter when the narration is supposed to be taken seriously:
"Cessez pourtant icy plus vous trupher et croyez qu'il n'est rien si vray que
l'Evangile" ("So now, stop laughing, and believe me that nothing is truer
than my tale, except the Gospel."). Thus Rabelais creates his own laughing
reader for this entire chapter composed of anecdotal proofs of *andouillicque*
virtue.

Readers of the novel recall also that the author-narrator mentions in his
letter to Monseigneur Odet, included in both editions of the *Quart Livre,*[6]
the fact that his benevolent readers got no small enjoyment and relief[7] from
his comic creation:

> plusiers gens langoureux, malades, ou autrement faschez et desolez, avoient,
> à la lecture d'icelles, trompé leurz ennuictz, temps joyeusement passé, et
> repceu alaigresse et consolation nouvelle.
>
> many dispirited, sick, and otherwise moping and sadly persons have escaped
> from their troubles for a cheerful hour or two, regained their spirits and taken
> fresh consolation by reading them.[8]

In this instance, we are on the edge of Rabelais's novel at the indistinct
limit where historical reality and literary fiction overlap. At times, Rabelais expands his narration to speak out across the abysm, creating a laughing public, but the establishment of clear-cut levels of narration in the four

books remains problematic. To grasp better the narrative act as it aims at laughter, it is necessary to consider for a moment the different kinds of narration as Joubert sees them and to distinguish between the fact and the content of narration.

For the theorist, comic narration is of two types: fables and anecdotes. Since he gives, respectively, examples of each, "les fables & contes facecieus, comme de Poge Florãtin, et les nouuelles de Bocace" ("fables and facetious tales, as from Poggio the Florentine, and the *novelle* of Boccaccio" [*TR,* 30]), the distinguishing feature is clear: fables, in the manner of Poggio, are about animals—with all too human traits—whereas anecdotes, or very short stories, as Boccaccio's *novelle,* treat beings and affairs explicitly human. To practice further division by saying that fables constitute fictitious narration and that anecdotes recount actual events would be forcing Joubert's illustration unduly.

We may think it strange that, rich in fables as Rabelais's novel is, none of the narrations is accompanied by laughter in the text, and only two laughers express the pleasure they take in anecdotes. A probable reason for the relatively small amount of mirth in and over a given narration, be it a fable or an anecdote, is simply due to the impracticality of interrupting a tight narrative sequence to introduce textual laughter. Whereas dialogue lends itself more naturally, by its piecemeal makeup, to the assignment of laughter to a given character, narration rejects such interruption.[9] Even the anecdotes that Joubert states to be the funniest, those dealing with cuckoldry, ". . . desquelles nous plaiset mieus pour rire, celles qui diet les tromperies faites des fames à leurs maris" (*TR,* 30), arouse little laughter in a novel that otherwise neglects no aspect of the subject, from Lasdaller's wife to the fervent quest of Panurge, from Frère Jan's syllogisms proving its inevitable presence to Rondibilis's Jovian remedy guaranteeing its absence. It can be said, paradoxically, that narration both draws and repels laughter. As we listen to a successful comic narration (one that brings about laughter), we save our laughter until the completion of the anecdote or an appropriate segment thereof.

It has been both possible and useful in previous analyses not to consider the narration of Rabelais-narrator (Alcofribas Nasier in *Pantagruel* and *Gargantua*) as *narration proper,* or *storytelling.* The term has been applied only to narration other than the author's, reserved to designate the recountings of a Panurge, an Epistemon, or a Bridoye. This means that Rabelais's narration must be taken as the background of reality upon which the stories of these other characters are played; it is to be compared to the impersonal relating of events by an objective eye that merely records the sequence of events. Even though such a supposition is diametrically opposed to the actual role of Rabelais as narrator, its justification is conceivable in light of the meager part the narrator has in the plot, especially in comparison with characters such as Pantagruel, Panurge, and Frère Jan; his presence is incidental and his support in the action is moral. One could even maintain that the presence of the narrator is no more than a feeble device making somewhat more feasible the repeated assertion on his part of the veracity of what is being related. This forceful assurance is necessary to his comic of hyperbolic guarantee, but limited nonetheless to such a function. As for the practice of addressing the reader, it can be seen as a rhetorical device used commonly in the literature of Antiquity, the Middle Ages, and the Renaissance.[10]

Turning toward some of the characters who laugh at the narration of anecdotes in the novel, we recall the episode of the *chevaux factices* in the twelfth chapter of *Gargantua*. The Seigneur de Painensac came to visit Grangousier in high fashion, *en gros train et apparat*. Now the giant's household was already fully engaged in receiving the duc de Francrepas and the comte de Mouillevent. This meant that the stables would not be able to accommodate all the horses, "le logis feut un peu estroict pour tant de gens, et singulierement les estables." What actually takes place as a result of this mundane overload is the subject of the chapter; the *maistre d'hostel* ("steward") and the *fourrier* ("outrider") of the Seigneur de Painensac, in search of more room for the visitors' horses, try to solve the logistical problem by asking the young Gargantua where the stables of the *grands chevaulx* might be. The ensuing dialogue, misunderstanding, and revelation of the child's character are comical in light of the author's intervention: "Devinez icy lequel des deux ilz avoyent plus matiere, ou de soy cascher pour leur honte, ou de rire pour le passetemps" ("Now how do you think they should have taken that? Should they have hung their heads for shame or laughed at the joke?"). The entire situation as actually experienced by the *maistre d'hostel* and the *fourrier* is recreated for the benefit of everyone present in Grandgousier's reception hall:

[Gargantua, the "maistre d'hostel" and the "fourrier"] entrerent en la salle basse où estoit toute la brigade, et, racontans ceste nouvelle histoire, les feirent rire comme un tas de mouches.

... entered the lower hall where all the company was; and when they told them this brand-new story, it made them laugh like a swarm of flies.[11]

The scene confirms in advance Joubert's category of narration because the recounting of the comic episode was successful in bringing about laughter. But one can rightly ask whether the laughter springs from the material recounted, from the fact of narration, or simply, and perhaps more reasonably, from the quality of narration.

No details are given concerning the style characterizing the narration of the Seigneur de Painensac's two domestics, but since the reader has just lived the entire scene, he can easily imagine such a recountal. Here is a case where the inner eye reconstitutes the *laughable in deed*. The laughers, *toute la brigade*, confirm a comic value. But this comic value, no longer that of the actual situation, is that of the narration of a past series of events, although very recent in this case, along with their comic interplay. Rabelais gives no definition of the constitutive parts or quality of a successful narration. He in fact does much better: the entire chapter is an illustration of such a narration. Although the temporary consideration of the episode as impersonal relation permits us to contemplate the chapter as the unfolding of a real-life happening, the reality remains nonetheless narrated. Actual fact has become comic art in and through the narration that is fixed textually and given the seal of laughter both internally and externally: internally when the two domestics laugh over the young Gargantua, and externally when the same scene, recounted by the two narrators, causes laughter among the listeners.

The reader is put on a par with the narrators inasmuch as he has just witnessed the entire sequence that they tell to *toute la brigade*. The result is an impression of reality, undoubtedly reinforced by the use of direct discourse. The chapter has thus an aura of what it is not: it appears to be a comical situation that the reader feels ready to relive, perhaps even to recount himself, to the guests in the reception hall. Rabelais, then, affords the reader no small pleasure in furnishing him with the illusion that he possesses the art of comic narration. The master narrator does this by making him associate with laughers who are successful in recreating comic reality, for characters in the novel who laugh and who make others laugh in narrating their laughable experiences tend to induce the same behavior on the part of the reader, *par sympathie naturelle*. In this chapter, Rabelais forces his laughter upon the reader, transforming him, inviting him to participate in the form of his own creation: that of a laugher-narrator.

There are, however, examples of laugh-provoking narrations that are less complex. An episode in the *Tiers Livre* could be called to the fore during which Carpalim takes great enjoyment in an anecdote narrated by Ponocrates:

> "— Monsieur nostre maistre, vous soyez le tresbien venu. J'ay prins moult grand plaisir vous oyant; et loue Dieu de tout."

> "My worthy master, . . . you are heartily welcome. I have greatly enjoyed listening to you, praise be to God for all good things."[12]

What Ponocrates recounted was a well-known novella. It had been re-popularized in a versified version as recently as 1535 by Gratien du Pont in his *Controverse des sexes masculin et feminin*. It is the story treating an extremely fashionable theme and matter for much debate in Rabelais's day: the inherent moral weakness of women. As Ponocrates narrates the anecdote, the reader does not fail to see its significance with regard to the plight of Panurge who is desperately in search of a chaste spouse—or more precisely the certitude that such a rarity exists. More important at the moment, however, is the fact that as a narration the account gives rise to laughter. It is the story of the nuns requesting the right to administer the sacrament of penance to one another in order to confess "quelque petites imperfections secretes, lesquelles honte insupportable leurs est deceler aux homes confesseurs" ("a few small secret imperfections, which it is unbearably shameful for them to reveal to male confessors"). To be emphasized here is that Carpalim's laughter is contingent upon Ponocrates's actual narration, even if the anecdote comes from the *Controverse* in a poetic form.

Although the anecdote may have been popular for several reasons at the time, its laughter-inciting virtues are confirmed historically only in and through Ponocrates's narration coupled with Carpalim's avowal of pleasure. Accordingly, Joubert's category receives corroboration by the anecdote only as it is narrated in Rabelais's novel. Had this little story remained at the versified stage that it had in Gratien du Pont's *Controverse,* the comic value of the anecdote, as well as the usefulness of Joubert's category, would not have gone beyond the realm of hypothesis.

Summary

The value of narration is both stated by Joubert and ratified by Rabelais. As a category of the comic, it draws heavily upon the subdivisions already discussed under the *laughable in deed*. An important result of Joubert's considering it as a division of the *laughable in word* is the diversion of our attention from the laughable to the inborn gifts of the narrator himself, and the setting of the laugher himself into an ever-sharpening focus.

Chapter 5

Laughter and Wordplay

WHEREAS NARRATION is able to share in all of the aspects of *laughter in deed*, wordplay seems to hinge principally upon the physical features of language:

> La propre matiere des propos ridicules, qui particulieremãt se raportet à l'ouye, et de ceus qu'on appelle brocars, lardons, irrisions, moqueries, mots piquans, mordans, equiuoques, ambigus, & qui retiret à deceptiõ, de quelle fasson que ce soit.

> The particular material of laughable speech is drawn from *brocars* (squibs, lampoons), *lardons* (taunts, sarcasm, gibes), *irrisions* (derision), *moqueries* (mockery, scoffing, ridicule), and remarks which are stinging, biting, equivocal, and which spring in any way from imposture. (*TR,* 30)

Yet the term that Joubert uses to designate this operation, *rancontrer,* indicates that more than mere sound is involved. In the sixteenth century this verb meant to joke or to make puns.[1] Etymologically it means to bring together or to meet.[2] An added meaning of meeting up with thieves[3] might suggest some result other than the purely physical combining of words; something is handed over in the encounter, and certain valuables are liberated from their former possessors. There is loss, exchange, gain. More than the mere rearranging of the concrete elements of language, wordplay has reverberations in the realm of the abstract.[4]

According to Joubert, these *rencontres,* almost numberless in their types, can be qualified morally:

> Or il y ha mille moyens de rancontrer, qui naisset des personnes, lieus, tams, & auantures fort diuerses: & sont an propos deshonetes, lascifs, facecieus, outrageus, facheus, niais, ou volages & indiscres.

> There are a thousand ways to make puns, based on people, places, periods, and diverse occurrences: and they take the form of remarks that are disgraceful, lascivious, facetious, outrageous, untimely, naive, fickle and indiscreet. (*TR,* 30)

But wordplay analyzed in terms of these eight moral epithets would not lead us to what is essential to their makeup. The mechanics of their construction is conceived of within the framework of rhetorical devices, or figures of speech:

> Leur forme principalle et, des figures d'oraison, ou manieres de parler communes aus Poëtes & Orateurs: comme d'amphibologie, enigme, cõparaison, metaphore, ficciõ, hyperbole, feintise, allegorie, emphase, beausemblant, dissimulation, & autres que mettet les Rhetoriciens. . . .

> They take their principal form from the figures of rhetoric, or manners of speaking common to poets and orators, such as amphibology, enigma, comparison, metaphor, fictio, hyperbole, pretence, allegory, emphasis (innuendo), beausemblant (form of allegory), and dissimulation, and others put forth by Rhetoricians. . . . (*TR,* 30–31)

Out of several hundred known rhetorical figures, Joubert gives special attention only to eleven of them, probably those most familiar to him.[5]

The fact that Joubert claims the figures of speech to be the basis of all wordplay is not without significance. In doing this, the theoretician removes from the realm of laws and absolute prescription the whole subject of the laughable and laughter. In a very real sense it is tantamount to denying the value of his categories of laughter: what had been cause is now either effect or circumstance. Just as the figures of speech are not actually governed by any preconceived set of rules, but rather defined or coded by their esthetic effect, which is itself caused by the spontaneity of thought or emotion, so also is laughter considered to be a vital prerogative of wordplay, expressing itself *in terms of* and *over* such external signs (puns), yet never taking its origin in them. In a word, laughter is not caused, but is the cause. Joubert studies these "effects," in this case, various examples of wordplay, couching them among the figures of speech to contemplate more easily their "cause." Effects, of course, never account wholly for the cause: the laughable is not responsible for laughter; laughter, rather, is responsible for the laughable.

But laughter is an abstraction unless it comes from the laugher, and this is precisely the merit of Joubert's treatise: he has dissected the laugher—man himself—and found laughter to be indissociably related to man's condition. Perceiver of opposed concepts, man is exposed to contrary emotions that in turn have their effect upon the heart. He thus restates for his times in physiological terms the formula of Aristotle: laughter both determines human nature and is determined by it.[6] So in terms of our discussion, although wordplay has a simple and almost mechanical origin, insofar as it begins by different arrangements of the physical elements of language, it carries along with each finding (*"inuantion"*) an added quality that has an appeal outside the area of linguistic manipulation. This added quality is what characterizes Joubert's category of wordplay: it is the role of the punster, as well as that of the laugher confronted by a pun, that now becomes pertinent.

Joubert's theory of the comic starts with laughter. It never loses sight of the physical source of laughter, the body of the laugher. His thought maintains a constant point of reference with the physiological framework of the senses and anatomy on the one hand, and the rhetorical tradition on the other, as he pursues the amplification of his theory. The main reason that the laugher's part in wordplay is more extensive than in any of the other contemporary theories is to be sought in Joubert's concentration on the vital relationship between the *rencontre,* or wordplay, and its source, the laughing punster. All this follows from the first movement of his thoughts on the comic. The cause of laughter cannot be dissociated from its effect:

"Lors nous disons etre impossible de randre plus euidãte la cause de leur effet, que la proprieté naturelle" (*TR,* 4). Thus Joubert carries with him this constant guide, a sort of idealized laugher, throughout his treatise.

What this means in terms of our discussion is that, for Joubert, wordplay is only an occasion of laughter, as are all the categories that he forms, and that laughter is principally an affair among laughers, accidentally occasioned by *deeds* and *words* around which laughers of a given period decide to laugh. In brief, men define the laughable more by their laughter and less with their reason.

As for wordplay in particular, Joubert believes that laughter surrounds these verbal exercises in the following way:

> Quãt à l'usage, nous faisons qu'on se rid, ou des autres, ou de nous mesmes: des autres, si an moquerie nous reprenons, refutons, meprisons, ou rabatons leur dire: de nous mesmes, quand nous disons quelque chose vn peu absurde, ou à notre eciant, ou sans y panser: & quand nous deceuons l'expectacion des ecoutans, ou que nous prenons les propos à rebours.

> As for their usage, we make these remarks so that others, or we ourselves, will be laughed at: others if in a mocking tone we take up, refute, mock, or abase what they say; ourselves when we say something a bit absurd, either on purpose or without thinking, and when we disappoint the expectation of the listeners or take what was said in the wrong way. (*TR,* 31)

The theoretician adds that the punster practices his craft without effort:

> On diroit, qu'an cela il n'y ha point d'artifice, & que tout (au moins le principal) git au naturel, & à l'occasion presante.

> One would say that it involves no artifice, and that everything (at least the principal) is spontaneous, and according to the present moment. (*TR,* 31)

Joubert refuses momentarily to concede that possessing a witty mind is wholly a gift bestowed by nature. He claims at first that making a "find" is not a question of inborn talent: "De-vray Nature ne fait pas seulement, qu'on soit habile ou subtil à l'inuancion" ("In truth it is not Nature alone that makes one clever or subtle in inventing puns"); but he ends up surrendering to the fact that the fundamental comic quality lies not in the pun, but in the one who comes up with it: "ains quelques vns se treuuet de telle grace & contenance à leur parler, qu'vn autre disant le mesme, ne seroit trouué si plaisant" ("but some have such grace and composure in their speech, that another saying the same thing, would not be considered as funny" [TR, 30–31]). From this it is not difficult to see that the ability to pun, rather than hinging upon the mastery of certain figures of rhetoric, is ultimately a matter of natural talent or inclination.

Equivocal Remarks

More hilarity in Rabelais's novel is over wordplay than over any other category of the laughable. Joubert, in harmony with the comic novelist's laughers, mentions the comic virtue of quick puns and equivocal remarks. He says there is laughter when we upset the expectation of the listeners, or when we take what is said the wrong way. Among the sundry puns over which mirth is spilled in the novel, readers recall Pantagruel's prolonged and powerful giggle after Panurge's play on words as he explains to the giant why the awesome thunderbolt would never fall upon walls raised up out of the *callibistrys des femmes*: " 'Ilz sont tous benists ou sacrez' " (" 'They are all blessed or consecrated' ").[7] The laughter is no doubt also in response to the grossness of Panurge's entire project. Joubert would call this *outrageus* (*TR*, 30). But aside from the moral aspect, it is wordplay over *benists ou sacrez* that triggers with immediacy Pantagruel's breathy guffaw; in French, both adjectives have the general meaning roughly the equivalent of *benoit*, or sacred. Lightning never strikes what is consecrated, according to the popular belief. But an added twist comes with the equivocal *sacrez*: as a substantive it means a bird of prey.[8] Henri II Estienne in his *Precellence du language françois* says that the *sacre* is a bird that gulps everything, scrubs everything, and scrapes everything.[9] Such a cross between the female *genitalia* and the sacred on the verbal level recalls Panurge's actual *tour* on the Parisian lady in church. Along with the ambiguity, one might at this point remember one of Joubert's subjects of laughter discussed earlier: during this episode, thanks to Panurge's fertile imagination, the giant *vient à decouurir les parties hôteuses*. But long before the wordplay begins, the desire to laugh on the part of the characters, in this case Panurge, steers the topic of conversation into an area favorable to laughter, if we accept Joubert's foremost category, the shameful parts.

Other puns turning around the same general subject are equally accompanied by outbursts of mirth. As the reader progresses through the remaining chapters of *Pantagruel,* he meets again the laughter of Pantagruel provoked by a witty *quiproquo* from Panurge, delivered in his usual bragadoccio manner. The expression *forma communa* borrowed from scholasticism[10] becomes equivocal, acquiring a *sens libre* in the context: " 'qu'il n'en eschappe pas une [putain] que je ne taboure en forme commune' " (" 'so that there remain not one [whore] that I in common form don't drum' "). Pantagruel's reaction is immediate: " '—Ha, ha, ha, dist Pantagruel.' "[11]

Still another of Joubert's *figures* is illustrated in Panurge's boastings: *l'hyperbole* qualified here as *lascive.*[12] The *gabs* continue as Eusthenes and Epistemon resort respectively to a vivid comparison and to a scriptural citation in order to express their amorous urges:

"— Et je, (dist Eusthenes), quoy, je ne dressay oncques puis que bougeasmes de Rouen, au moins que l'aiguille montast jusques sur les dix ou unze heures, voire encores que l'aye dur et fort comme cent diables.
— Vrayement, (dist Panurge), tu en auras des plus grasses et des plus refaictes.
— Comment, (dist Epistemon), tout le monde chevauchera et je meneray l'asne. Le diable emporte qui en fera rien. Nous userons du droict de guerre: *Qui potest capere capiat.*"

"And I too," said Eusthenes, "I've never had a stand since we left Rouen, at least not so much of one that my needle went up to ten or eleven o'clock. So now it's hard and strong as a thousand devils."
"Indeed you shall have some of the fattest and those in best condition," said Panurge.
"What," cried Epistemon. "Is all the world to ride and I to lead the ass? Devil take the man who does that! We'll observe the right of war: *Qui potest capere capiat.*"[13]

Panurge, in reply to Epistemon's complaint, participates fully in the verbal banter: " '— Non, non, (dist Panurge), mais atache ton asne à un croc et chevauche comme le monde' " (" 'No, no," said Panurge, "tie your ass to a stump and ride like the rest' "). Although two of Joubert's divisions, *comparaison* and *mots equivoques,* are ratified by Pantagruel's laughter, it is Panurge who expresses what was to become the theorist's favorite comic device:

i'estime la plus facecieuse, de sauoir randre mansonge pour mansonge, &
pour le ridicule vn samblable bien à-propos. . . . nous faisons qu'on se rid . . .
si an moquerie nous reprenons . . . leur dire.

I esteem the most facetious to know how to render a lie for a lie, and for
something funny a similar reply in the same connection. . . . we cause others
to laugh . . . if we take up in jest their words. (*TR*, 31)

The proof of the actual comic value of the whole conversation is the giant's
laughter, approving the entire scene: "Et le bon Pantagruel ryoit à
tout. . . ." The laughing giant himself then makes use of the same device,
but his mood becomes resolutely sober if not grim:

"Vous comptez sans vostre hoste. J'ay grand peur que, devant qu'il soit
nuyct, ne vous voye en estat que ne aurez grande envie d'arresser, et qu'on
vous chevauchera à grand coup de picque et de lance."

"You're reckoning without your host, . . . I'm very much afraid that before
night falls I may see you in such a state that you'll have no great desire to
stand up. You are more likely to be battered down with great blows of the
pike and lance."

Now the events take on a very different appearance, confirming in turn
Joubert's general comic theory concerning emotional involvement, which
the theoretician states in the following manner:

si d'auanture an premier nous rions, ignorans le dommage, finalemant de
telle cognoissance frappés à compassion, nous quittons le Ris antieremāt,
& disons an repantance, il n'y ha pas dequoy rire: tant sont necessairemāt
iointes ces deus condicions, laideur & faute de pitié.

if perchance at first we laugh, not knowing the injury, eventually struck to
compassion by such knowledge, we cease laughing altogether, and say in
repentance that there is nothing to laugh about: so closely joined are these
two conditions, ugliness and lack of pity. (*TR*, 18)

The laugh-impeding aspect of serious concern, so well expressed by

Bergson in his remarks on the comic fall, had already acquired a solid tradition in French comic theory in Boileau and Joubert, before going back to Aristotle.[14]

Spiritual Remarks

But laughter is never far off in Rabelais's novel. A simple pun from a simple mind brings about the following self-approving victorious laugh, which readers of Rabelais will immediately recognize:

> "*Omnis clocha clochabilis, in clocherio clochando, clochans clochativo clochare facit clochabiliter clochantes. Parisius habet clochas. Ergo gluc.*
> Ha, ha, ha, . . ."[15]

The famous *ergo gluc* concludes abruptly the absurd reasoning, in mock Latin, of the ringing bells, but it is also a play on words. The term *gluc,* recalling the German word for bell, *glocke,* comes as a final note to silence emphatically the sophist's argument. Indeed, Janotus is one whom the French would not hesitate to call, precisely in this instance, a *cloche.* Janotus's laughing over his own wordplay confirms again the favorite type of *laughable in word* in Joubert's system: taking up in another way—in this case in German—one's own proposals is the most amusing, *la plus facecieuse,* figure of speech (*TR,* 31). It is closely related to repetition, or emphasis, which Joubert lists as the ninth figure and circumstance of laughter under wordplay. Janotus's laughter, although reflecting his hollow narcissism, is singularly rich in its correspondence to a contemporary esthetic opinion on puns.

In another instance, a titter of laughter from some young girls follows Homenaz's reaction to Gymnaste's incredible but well-received story of the arrow that defied the laws of nature rather than pierce one page of a canon law text, sacrilegiously used as a target:

> "— Miracle, s'escria Homenaz, miracle, miracle! Clerice, esclaire icy. Je boy à tous. Vous me semblez vrays Christians."
> A ces motz les filles commencerent ricasser entre elles.

"A miracle!" cried Greatclod, "a miracle, a miracle! Here, clerk, bring me a light. I drink to you all. You seem good Christians to me."

When they heard this, the girls began to giggle among themselves.[16]

Accompanying Homenaz's mirth, besides the general wine-inspired exuberance discussed elsewhere by Joubert, is the *emphase* just mentioned above as he thrice repeats his "miracle," the doubly equivocal *clerice, esclaire icy,* and finally the more subtle *vrays Christians,* which is geographically, so to speak, closest in the text to the actual laughter of the young girls. We have just seen the comic value of emphasis and repetition.[17] As for the double pun on *clerice esclaire icy,* there is the Latin word for clerk, which, in the vocative case, *clerice,* is roughly homophonic with the French *esclaire icy.* This expression means to bring light to a text. One easily imagines the people of the times calling upon a clerk to read, explain, or perhaps even to interpret a text. A strictly literal reading is also possible: to bring the light closer. This is based upon Homenaz's repetition of his play on words: "'Clerice, dist Homenaz, Clerice, esclaire icy à double lanternes'" ("'Clerk,' cried Greatclod, 'Clerk, get some light here, and make it two lanterns' ").[18] The pun becomes not only double when Homenaz uses the fixed expression to call for more wine, *clairet,* but perhaps also triple, if the *Decretaliste* is aware of the *vertu inspiratrice* of such wine inspiring or "clarifying" the proposed explanation. Rabelais's labyrinthine puns underscore and confirm Joubert's choice of *mots equivoques* as occasions of laughter.

Homenaz's final exclamation just before the girls begin to laugh is his *Vous me semblez vrays Christians* delivered at what must be full amplitude. This statement is addressed in loud candor to a group that is obviously composed of Christians; the mere presence of Frère Jan heightens the blatancy of this overexuberance. This same instance thus gives more weight to Joubert's division of *propos . . . niais* under the *laughable in word.* Any subtleties rumbling under the arrant simplicity of Homenaz's crystal utterance should be attributed to the girls as they snicker upon realizing that the relationship between the *brigade* and *Decretaliste* is not one to one; their playful deceit in furnishing Homenaz with anecdotes that enhance the glory and power of Canon Law is scarcely Christian. The wordplay, in this case accidental, given the naïveté of the theologian, does not go without corroborating once again another of Joubert's divisions under wordplay, that of taking words in a different sense, "ou que prenons les propos à rebours," while the light hypocrisy substantiates the seventh and the eleventh *figures* Joubert lists, *feintise* and *dissimulation*. All of these are ratified by the young girls' laughter.

Among the *comparaisons* (third figure cited by Joubert) spurring hilarity, readers of Rabelais recall the paralleled antitheses uttered by Panurge in chapter XIV of *Pantagruel,* just after the awesome resolution of Baisecul's and Humevesne's difference. All are celebrating with the wine offered to Pantagruel as a token of admiration. Panurge excels in swallowing no small quantity:

> "ce vin est fort bon et bien delicieux, mais plus j'en boy, plus j'ai de soif. Je croy que l'ombre de Monseigneur Pantagruel engendre les alterez, comme la lune faict les catharres."

> "This wine is very good and most delicious, but the more I drink of it the thirstier I am. I believe that the shadow of my lord Pantagruel makes men thirsty, as the moon makes catarrhs."[19]

Although several goblets of wine might be responsible for a considerable backlog of mirth, it is the striking parallel of two opposed causes and their two respective and opposite effects that unleashes the crowd's merriment: "Auquel commencerent rire les assistans." But it is what follows this particular occurrence of laughter that is of special interest, since it is an illustration in advance of Joubert's theory that he who makes others laugh is himself a laugher: "Ce que voyant, Pantagruel dist: 'Panurge, qu'est ce que avez à rire?' " Here it is clearly seen in the text that Panurge the punster participates in the laughter engendered.

Another comparison, in sharp contrast to the one just noted above, comes in chapter XXIV of the *Tiers Livre.* This incident calls for attention because its subject is laughter; yet no laughter graces it. Panurge, deep in the throes of doubt about his vocation in life and receiving counsel from his companion Epistemon, still finds the wherewithal to make a pun as his friend compares the playful bathos style of Enguerrant to the age-old image of a mountain giving birth to a mouse:

> "La mocquerie est telle que de la montaigne d'Horace, laquelle crioyt et lamentoyt enormement, comme femme en travail d'enfant. A son cris et

lamentation accourut tout le voisinage, en expectation de veoir quelque admirable, et monstrueux enfantement, mais enfin ne naquist d'elle qu'une petite souriz.
— Non pourtant (dist Panurge) je m'en soubrys."

"It is all as comical as Horace's mountain, that cried out and groaned so much, like a woman in labour. At its cries and lamentations all the neighbors ran up, expecting to see some marvellous and monstrous childbirth; but all that she produced in the end was a little mouse."
"It'll take more than your mouse to make me laugh," exclaimed Panurge.

The fact that Panurge does not laugh at his wordplay *souriz-soubrys* after Epistemon's comparison of Panurge's multiplying of difficulties in his quandary over marriage does not mean that this passage is in contradiction to Joubert's theory. On the contrary, one can see in this worn anecdote not only an illustration of his division of visual disappointment already discussed, but also further substantiation of his general theory. Panurge is too involved emotionally to laugh:

"Ainsi feray comme porte mon veu. Or, long temps a que avons ensemble, vous et moy, foy et amitié jurée par Juppiter Philios. Dictes m'en vostre advis: me doibs je marier ou non?"

"I shall do as my vow impels me. Long ago we swore faith and friendship together by Jupiter Philios, you and I. Now give me your advice. Ought I to marry or not?"[20]

Neither the pun nor the comparison occasions laughter, yet Joubert's theory accounts for the absence of mirth in this passage. In this particular case, Panurge's lack of laughter bolsters the Aristotelian aspect of Joubert's general theory.

Which Came First?

As we have mentioned above, Joubert's theory seems perplexing in that laughter may also be seen as the source of wordplay rather than resulting from it. Some of Rabelais's laughers validate this conception as well. In the

episode where Frère Jan takes friendly advantage of Gymnaste's equally
friendly gibe in chapter XL of *Gargantua,* the monk is told that a drop is
hanging from his runny nose: "Gymnaste luy dist: 'Frere Jean, oustez ceste
rouppie que vous pend au nez'" ("'Friar John,' said Gymnaste, 'wipe off
that drip that's hanging on your nose'"). His laughter precedes the pun,
seeming to provide the energy necessary for the verbal creation. But the
energy is far from expended, for Frère Jan continues to expound on his
rather large nose, answering his own rhetorical question:

> "—Ha! ha! (dist le moyne) serois je en dangier de noyer, veu que suis en
> l'eau jusques au nez? Non, non. *Quare? Quia* elle en sort bien, mais poinct
> n'y entre, car il est bien antidoté de pampre. O mon amy, qui auroit bottes
> d'hyver de tel cuir, hardiment pourroit il pescher huytres, car jamais ne
> prendroient eau."

> "Ha, ha!" said the monk, "am I not in danger of drowning, seeing that
> I'm in water up to the nose? No, no, *quare? Quia* (why? Because)
> It goes not in as water, though as water it may come out,
> For it's properly corrected with grape-juice antidote. O my friend, anyone
> who had winter boots of such leather could boldly fish for oysters, for they
> would never let in water."[21]

Comparaisons or *metaphores* and *autres que mettet les Rhetoriciens* (*TR,* 31)
abound in the merry exuberance following the microcosmic drop. Here the
laughter seems to generate the verbal sport, thus pointing to Joubert's
conception of laughter preceding wordplay.

Pantagruel touches on this idea in the *Quart Livre* when he tells how
Cicero's mocking laughter generated lampoons to strengthen the tired
morale of the Pompeians:

> Un jour entendent que les Pompeians à certaine rencontre avoient faict
> insigne perte de leurs gens, voulut visiter leur camp. En leur camp apperceut
> peu de force, moins de couraige, et beaucoup desordre. Lors praevoyant que
> tout iroit à mal et perdition, comme depuis advint, commença trupher et
> mocquer maintenant les uns, maintenant les aultres, avecques brocards
> aigres et picquans, comme très bien sçavoit le style. Quelques capitaines,
> faisans des bons compaignons comme gens bien asceurez et deliberez, luy
> dirent: "voyez vous combien nous avons encore d'aigles?" C'estoit lors la

devise des Romains en temps de guerre. "Cela, respondit Ciceron, seroit bon
et à propos si guerre aviez contre les pies."

Hearing one day that the Pompeians had lost a considerable number of men
in a certain engagement, he decided to visit their camp. There he found little
strength, less courage, and great disorder. Foreseeing, therefore, that they
would be utterly ruined and destroyed—as indeed was the case—he began to
jibe and mock, first at one party, then at another, making those bitter and
stinging observations at which he was such an adept. Some of the captains,
being stout, resolute, and confident fellows, took his mockery in good part
and replied: "But don't you see how many eagles we've still got?" Eagles
were then the Roman ensigns in time of war. "They would be good and
useful if you were fighting against magpies." answered Cicero.[22]

Cicero's invincible spiritual health provided the comic force necessary to
forge his witty reply.

Another illustration of this notion is met in Panurge's recounting of
Breton Villandry's clever reply to the "duc de Guyse." It seems that Breton, majestically armed and exquisitely mounted, was not seen on the field
of combat. When he boldly states that he was where even the duke himself
would not have dared to be seen, the latter flared up in anger:

> Le seigneur duc prenant en mal ceste parolle, comme trop brave et teme-
> rairement proferée, et se haulsant de propous, Breton facilement en grande
> risée l'appaisa, disant: "J'estois avecque le baguaige: on quel lieu vostre
> honneur n'eust soy cacher comme je faisois."

The noble Duke considered this speech both rash and a good deal too
insolent and, somewhat offended, broke off the conversation. But Breton
easily calmed him down by saying, to the general amusement: "Yes, I was
with the baggage, a place in which your Grace would never have dared to
hide, as I did."[23]

Here it is even more evident that Breton's laughter fathers his *inuantion*. It
is clear that his quick twist ("*avecques le baguaige*") was successful in quiet-
ing if not amusing the duke, thus corroborating once again one of Joubert's
divisions under wordplay: "nous faisons qu'on se rid . . . quand nous dece-
vons l'expectacion des ecoutãs" (*TR,* 31).

Another example is found in chapter XXVII of *Pantagruel*. Panurge effects a burlesque transfer of Pantagruel's *dicton victorial* to the kitchen level whereupon Epistemon, with a wide smile, takes the very mold of the giant's rhetorical exhortation on bravery and recasts it playfully into a culinary form:

> Lors dist Pantagruel:
> "Allons, enfans, c'est trop musé icy à la viande, car à grand poine voit on advenir que grans bancqueteurs facent beaulx faictz d'armes. Il n'est umbre que d'estandartz, il n'est fumée que de chevaulx et clycquetys que de harnoys."
> A ce commencza Epistemon soubrire et dist:
> "Il n'est umbre que de cuisine, fumée que de pastez et clicquetys que de tasses."
>
> Then said Pantagruel: "Come my lads, we have brooded here too long on our victuals. It is no easy thing, as we know, for great feasters to perform great deeds of arms. But there is no shade like that of banners, there is no smoke like that of the horses, nor clattering like that of armour."
> At this Epistemon began to smile and said: "There is no shade like that of kitchens, no smoke like pie-smoke, and no clattering like that of cups."[24]

Again, the hilarity can be seen here as a prerogative to the wordplay. This particular kind of humor is especially appreciated by Joubert, and Panurge's clever casting made in the same mold would have doubtlessly pleased the theoretician for whom the shameful parts have much comic worth.[25]

A final instance, still concerning Epistemon and Pantagruel, is found in chapter LXIII of the *Quart Livre*. Having set out to sea, the band joyfully continues its quest. Near the island of Chaneph, however, the waves disappear and the sails become windless. The companions and crew, less merry than usual, try to pass the time. Suddenly Pantagruel breaks the dull silence with a pun on stirring up the stagnant atmosphere, both with regards to the weather and the dead calm on board:

> Adoncques rompant cestuy tant obstiné silence, à haulte voix, en grande alaigresse d'esprit, demanda: "Maniere de haulser le temps en calme?"

Then, breaking this obstinate silence, he asked in a loud voice and in the gayest of spirits: "What's the best way to raise fine weather in the doldrums?"[26]

Epistemon, rather gifted in this sort of wordplay, follows suit in a manner heralding more than one of Joubert's ideas on the subject: "Epistemon tierça en guayeté de coeur, demandant: 'Maniere de uriner? la personne n'en estant entalentée'" ("Epistemon came in third with the light-hearted inquiry: 'How can a man make water when he has no urge to?'"). Both characters are precharged with merriment as they send forth their bolts of wit, but Epistemon approaches the level of a virtuoso in furnishing a crackling burst of phonemic sparks in his *finale* "n'en estant entalentée."

Nor does the level of ideas receive less attention: the answer to the posed riddle is immediate. Urinating *par naturelle sympathie,* much as Rhizotome spreads his contagious yawn, is seen as the solution:

> Rhizotome estoit acropy sus le coursouoir. Adoncques levant la teste et profondement baislant, si bien qu'il, par naturelle sympathie, excita tous ses compaignons à pareillement baisler, demanda: "Remede contre les oscitations et baislements?"

> Rhizotome, who was squatting on the gangway, then raised his head and, yawning so widely as to cause all his friends to yawn also out of natural sympathy, he demanded: "What's the remedy for oscitation or yawning?"

Yawning, urinating, and laughter, *affliccions* that are spread by *occulte sympathie de Nature* according to Rabelais's laughers, are all conceived of in identical terms by the theoretician. This is brought out when Joubert puts the case of a man who, ignorant of the cause of mirth among others, still, by a natural sympathy, feels compelled to laugh upon witnessing their hilarity:

> Et si d'auanture il se met à rire, ce sera bien à credit, & d'un accord[b] naturel [marginal note: "b Come de voir balher on balhe: & quelquefois on pisse par cōpagnie."], qui souuant nous incite (mouuans les appetis) à imiter noz sãblables. . . .

> And if perchance he begins to laugh, it will certainly be upon credit, and of a natural accord[b] [marginal note: "b As when seeing another yawn, we yawn: and sometimes we piss for company's sake."], which often incites us (by moving our appetites) to imitate our fellowmen. . . .(TR, 37)

Thus the remedy prescribed in the case of a lack of laughter is *compagnie*, but a *compagnie* where laughter already reigns. The cause of the self-perpetuating yawn is as unknown as that of the self-perpetuating laugh: "Pourquoy est-ce, que si quelqu'un viẽt à baalher, à peine les voyãs s'an peuuet contenir?" ("Why is it that if somebody happens to yawn, those seeing him are scarcely able to keep from doing it?" [TR, 5]).

Laughter, then, is seen here to be a free force, or at least a preexisting one. It is not the child of cause, but is rather the father of an effect: wordplay. This wordplay, according to Joubert as well as in Rabelais, may be read as the expression of a self-sufficient laughter that is creative. In this sense, laughter is godlike in Rabelais and not diabolic as it is for Baudelaire.[27] In the sixteenth century one of the expressions of its vital energy is the engendering of wordplay. To see these puns as *pointed* fabrications, sharpened and aimed at certain abuses, is to miss a great portion of both their real direction and their source. They come from a self-sufficient authorial laughter, or laugher, and are directed as means of communication or expression of this invented personality to the reader. The laughter is fictitious; any connection, therefore, with real persons or events is accidental or tangential—which is not to say, however, that it is unintentional. But the real comic lifeblood goes to the reader. The few drops (or gigantic gallons) seen to spill over onto contemporary matters are incidental, even if the modern reader is less used to such blood than was his sixteenth-century counterpart.

Summary

The category of wordplay is well bolstered by Rabelais's laughers. Of the eleven *figures* listed, only three missed the approval of Rabelaisian mirth. Five of the eight moral qualities of the *rancontres* are attributable to characters' puns. This category, although being the more developed and having the greater number of ramifications under the *laughable in word,* is at the same time the poorest in examples of *ridenda.* Perhaps we are to believe that the theoretician, lacking in comic genius, sought refuge in theory—a sort of Sainte-Beuve *avant la lettre*. Or did he simply feel uncomfortable in citing puns outside of their vital context: the laughter of *compagnie?*

Even the internal stability of the treatise itself is uncertain. Joubert seems to fluctuate between considering laughter as a cause or as an effect. Rabelais's laughers, although remaining blissfully unconcerned about the theoretical plight, indicate by their very laughter that Joubert was profoundly right in experiencing discomfort over the real nature of his subject of investigation. Although frequently using terms such as *causes* and *effais,* Joubert was keenly aware that, in wordplay, he was really only dealing with concomitants of laughter.[28] Through his categories and divisions—constantly sounded out by Rabelais's relentless mirth—we gain insight into those aspects of an eternal question that was crucial in the eyes, ears, and hearts of sixteenth-century laughers.

Chapter 6

Joubert's Epithets
of Laughter and
Rabelais's Laughers

THE GREAT MOMENTS of creation and recreation in man's life are accompanied by intense pleasure; procreation, repast, and spiritual regeneration are all marked by a joy that draws him to participate in the continuance of his own kind. Rabelais's characters often bear witness to the joy-engendering aspects of fabricating both the corporeal and the social life-blood. Joubert, speaking more specifically about the pleasure inherent in laughter as it replenishes the spirits, even likens it to a sovereign good:

l'acte nous est fort agreable, & le souhaitons fort affectueusemant, pour le plaisir qu'il denote. Car nous auons naturellemāt telle affecciō à reiouissance, que tous nos desseins y pretandet, cõme à un souuerain bien.

the act is enjoyable to us, and we desire it very deeply for the pleasure that characterizes it. For we have such a natural penchant for enjoyment that all of our designs are aimed at it, as a sovereign good. (*TR*, 8)

Yet Joubert realized also that laughter, besides being subject to misuse (an entire chapter of the second book of the treatise is entitled "Du Ris mal-sain, & batard" ["On Unhealthy and Bastard Laughter"]), has as many facets as the manifold personalities of Everyman. In the seventh chapter of the second book, the theorist furnishes descriptions of some particular kinds of laughter commonly spoken of during the times. Here laughter is seen to share in the diversity of man himself, showing the distinctness of each facet. Few who write on the subject seem struck so sharply by the almost infinite number of forms laughter assumes during the Renaissance as Joubert. It is one of the most *amirables accions de l'homme* and has as many manifestations as there are individuals:

> An l'espece des hommes il y ha autant de visages differans, qu'il y ha de figures au monde: autant de diversités, tant au parler, que à la vois, & (s'il vous plait) autãt de divers Ris.

> In the species of man there are as many different faces as there are heads in the world: as much diversity in speech as in voice, and (if you will) as much diverse laughter. (*TR,* 210)

His description of its diverse types borders on poetry. Some men, writes Joubert, sound like geese hissing when they laugh and others, like grumbling goslings. Some recall the sigh of woodland pigeons, or doves in their widowhood and others, the hoot-owl. One might be like an Indian rooster and another, like a peacock. Others give out a peep-peep, like chicks. From others comes a sound like a horse neighing, an ass heehawing, a hog snorting, or a dog yapping or choking. Some people call to mind the sound of dry-axled carts and still others, gravel in a pail, and others yet, a boiling pot of cabbage, "vne potée de chous qui bout" (*TR,* 211).

But here Joubert interrupts himself to say that a complete listing would be as impossible as it would be useless, for each may observe the infinite variety of laughter, "chacun peut à part soy observer infinies sortes & manieres de Ris." He announces his intention to list only the main differences and principal epithets, so the reader might become familiar with the terms:

> Nous n'avons intancion que d'ajouter aus devant-dittes, les differances accidantales, & les principaus epithetes du Ris, qu'on lit ez bõs auteurs: à fin que chacun antande leur sinificacion.

We have the intention of adding to the above-mentioned only differences of accident, and the principal epithets of laughter which are read among good authors, in order that each might understand their sense. (*TR*, 212)

Types of Laughter

Joubert's list of epithets begins with what he considers a particularly fitting term, *Ris trāblāt,* inasmuch as the trembling of the voice is the essence of true laughter as discussed in his first book. The *Ris trāblāt* is subdivided into *Ris modeste* and *Ris cachin:* modest laughter is that already treated in the first book, whereas *cachinnation,* far from being ordinary, is "immodeste, deborde, insolant & trop long, qui romt les forces" ("immodest, excessive, insolent, overly long, and depletes our strength" [*TR,* 213]). The theoretician likens *cachinnation* to what the Greeks called *Ris syncrousien* because it rumbles and shakes violently, *de ce qu'il crole & ebranle fort.* The laughter that Joubert taxes with the rather depreciative term *Agriogele* is related to the *Ris cachin* since he defines it as that of the blabbermouth: "du jaseur et bavard, qui se plait an bourdes & toutes badineries, riant temerairemant, sans avoir ou tenir contenance" ("of the jabberer and talkative one, who enjoys nonsense and every kind of trifle, laughing temerariously and keeping no composure"[*TR,* 218–19]). Yet because it is less violent than *cachinnation,* it is to be associated with the *Ris modeste* or visualized somewhere in between the *Ris cachin* and the *Ris Ionique,* which is also known as the *Ris-chien, de Chio*—not to be confused with the *Ris canin,* which is discussed below. All share one common quality: they are well-intentioned. The *Ris Ionique,* or *Ris-chien,* is the least intense of those discussed thus far:

... propre aus mous, delicas & adonnés à leurs plaisirs, car on ha taxé les delices des Ioniens antre les Grecs, comme la pompe, superfluité, mignardise & mollesse des Sybarites antre les Barbares. A maimes sans on dit *Ris-chien, de Chio,* Ile de grands delices.

... proper to the soft, delicate, and given over to pleasure, for the Ionians among the Greeks are accused of delights, as are the Sybarites among the Barbarians of pomp, superfluousness, delicacy and weakness. In a similar sense one speaks of "*Ris-chien,*" of Chio, island of great delights. (*TR,* 218)

To be grouped together also are the types of ill-intentioned laughter. Beginning with the most vehement form mentioned by Joubert, there is the *Ris Ajacin,* the roaring and devouring lionlike laughter of Ajax:

> . . . allant cõbatre cors à cors, ou an duël: dont aussi on l'ha appellé depuis an-sa, Ris *Ajacin,* quand on rit de rage, felonie, & mal-talant. Hesiode ecrit de Iupiter, qu'il rit de maime, etant courroucé à l'ancontre de Promethee, pour luy avoir prins furtivemant du feu. On l'estime aussi fatal, quand le dangier et imminant à quelqu'vn, lors qu'il se rit & se joüe, plongé an voluptés malefices.

> . . . going to hand to hand combat, or to a duel: for which reason it has since been called Ris *Ajacin* when one laughs out of rage, crime, and evil intent. Hesiod writes that Jupiter laughed in this manner when he was angry upon meeting Prometheus over the fire he had stolen from him. It is also considered inevitable, when someone is in imminent danger, to laugh and frisk while plunged in voluptuousness or evil-doing. (*TR,* 217)

More tempered, but still full of *mal-talant,* is the *Ris Sardonien,* more commonly called *Ris d'Hotelier.* This is the laughter of those who are outwardly merry but inwardly distilling black malice:

> On vse de ce mot, *Ris Sardonien,* à l'androit de ceus qui contrefont les joyeus, ayans martel an taite, outrés de facherie: & qui d'vne caresse voilet & couvret leur mal-veulhance. Tel Ris et manteur, simulé & traitre, plein d'amertume & mal-talãt, ou (pour le moins) de feintise: duquel on fait beau-samblant, à celuy qu'on n'aime point: cõme le Ris qu'on dit vulgairemant *d'Hotelier.*

> The word *Ris Sardonien* is used in the case of those who feign to be joyous while bearing a club in their mind, exasperated by anger, and who veil and cover their ill will with a caress. Such laughter is mendacious, counterfeit and traitorous, full of bitterness and evil intent, or (at least) affectedness, from which one forms a semblance of pleasantness for somebody one detests, like the laughter commonly called *d'Hotelier* (inn-keeper). (*TR,* 214)

Still less intense is the *Ris canin,* which derives its name from dogs, according to the following *metaphore*:

Nous avons touché le Ris canin, lequel et ainsi dit, de ce que le rieur decouvre seulemãt les dans. La metaphore ou trãslacion et prise des chiẽs, qui ont celà pour sine de courrous, de moutrer les dans. Car tel et le Ris de ceus, qui ne riet du coeur.

We have touched upon the Ris canin, which is so called because the laugher only uncovers the teeth. The metaphor or transference is taken from dogs, who as a sign of anger show their teeth. For such is the laughter of those who do not laugh from the heart. (*TR, 216*)

Least intense, finally, is the *Ris Megarique*. Overcome by sadness, distress, or anger, only a faint smile signals the presence of this "Ris feint & contrefait" ("feigned and counterfeit laughter") "quand on rit etant marry antieremant" ("when one laughs when completely dejected" {*TR, 215–17*}).

Last of the types of laughter listed by Joubert are those that all share a common characteristic trait: the lack of cause. "*Le Ris sans cause, et sine de sotie. . . . Risus sine re, signũ est stultitiae*" ("Laughter without cause is a sign of madness" {*TR, 173*}), writes the theoretician. Again, the most agitated form is the *Ris Catonien:*

. . . lequel et fort debordé & ebranlant. Car on dit, que Caton le Sanseur, ne rit jamais de sa vie qu'vne fois, & que lors il rit excessivemant, quand il vit vn ane manger des chardons: & qu'etant tout rompu de rire, il s'ecria, ces laivres ont de samblables laituës.

. . . which is most excessive and upsetting. For it is said that Cato the censor never laughed in his life but one time, and he then laughed excessively, when he saw an ass eating thistles; and completely broken by laughter, he cried out that these lips have similar lettuce. (*TR, 218*)

How the censor's laugh-infested remarks relate to the thistle-eating donkey remains unknown, whence the term *sine re*. Next comes the *Ris Thorybode*, less strong than Catonic laughter, but still characterized by convulsions: "Nous avõs parlé cy dessus du Ris tumultueus, qu'Hyppocras appelle *Thorybode*, lequel n'et point legitime, ains de convulsion" ("We have spoken above of the *Ris tumultueus*, which Hippocrates called *Thorybode*, and which is not legitimate, but convulsionary" {*TR, 219*}). The most serene form of senseless mirth is named *Ris Inepte*. This would be a keyed-down *fou rire*. Here ends Joubert's list of epithets, which might be summarized according to the following schema:

		OCCASION		
		GOOD OR WELL-INTENTIONED	EVIL OR ILL-INTENTIONED	MAD OR UNCAUSED
INTENSITY	EXCESSIVE	Ris cachin	Ris Ajacin	Ris Catonien
	STRONG	Ris Agriogele	Ris Sardonien (*d'Hotelier*)	Ris *Thorybode*
	MEDIUM	Ris modeste	Ris canin	
	WEAK	Ris Ionique	Ris megaric (soub-ris)	Ris *Inepte*

Good Laughter in Rabelais

Socrates is the first laugher that Rabelais presents. As he appears in the prologue to *Gargantua,* Socrates would incite laughter on the basis of Joubert's theory because of his ugliness: "tant laid il estoit de corps et ridicule en son maintien" ("so ugly was his body and so absurd his appearance"). As a laugher he would be placed among the more robust. The problem arises when one tries to settle on the type. Even though there is an aspect of dissimulation, "toujours dissimulant son divin sçavoir" ("always concealing his divine wisdom"), it is to be seen as a well-intentioned and humble veiling of his omniscience rather than a calculating *Ris d'Hotelier*. One might attempt to tax him with the *Ris Catonien* of a maniac on the basis of his haggard appearance, "le reguard d'un taureau, le visaige d'un fol" ("the stare of a bull, the face of a fool"), but such an endeavor becomes pointless under the weight of his sane and sober qualities; he had "entendement plus que humain, vertus merveilleuse, couraige invincible, sobresse non pareille, contentement certain, asseurance parfaicte" ("a superhuman understanding, miraculous virtue, invincible courage, unrivalled sobriety, unfailing contentment, perfect confidence"). He was also sociable, although certainly not mundane: "toujours riant, toujours beu-vant d'autant à un chascun, toujours se guabelant" ("always laughing, always drinking glass for glass with everybody, always playing the fool"). Only two of the theoretician's epithets seem to qualify him at this point, both under the *well-intentioned* rubric: *Ris cachin* and *Ris Agriogele*. The final choice must hesitate timelessly between rowdy laughter and the *Agriogele*. There is perhaps more than we realize of the guffawing farmer in this Socrates: "simple en meurs, rustiq en vestimens, pauvre de fortune, . . . inepte à tous offices de la republique, toujours riant" ("simple in manners, rustic in clothing, poor in fortune, . . . unfit for all public duties, always laughing").[1] But this is a sixteenth-century Socrates, transformed and illustrated by Rabelais. Joubert would never have cast the Greek philosopher in such light material. In his mind Socrates is not at all *hilare:*

> On dit aussi de Socrate (tres-renommé pour sa grande sagesse) qu'il etoit toujours de maime visage, ne plus joyeus, ne plus troublé.

> It is also said of Socrates (very renowned for his great wisdom) that he always had the same look, neither joyful nor troubled. (*TR,* 250)

Although the manifold qualities of the first of Rabelais's laughers permit him to dance lightly across Joubert's field of epithets, further analysis does limit the possibilities of attribution. This not only proves the usefulness of the theoretician's types, but also enhances our knowledge of Rabelais's Socrates: he is transformed into a laugher by the novelist.

Other laughers in the novel who seem to corroborate this sort of hilarity are numerous. There is Pantagruel as he questions the narrator on the subject of his daily relief during his stay in the giant's mouth:

> "—Voire mais, (dist il), où chioys tu?
> — En vostre gorge, Monsieur, dis je."

> "Indeed," said he, "and where did you shit?" "In your throat, my lord," said I.

The reaction might well have been one of thunderous wrath, but although possessing many times the strength of Ajax, the lumbering Pantagruel has none of the shieldbearer's ferocity in his laughter:

"— Ha, ha, tu es gentil compaignon, (dist il). Nous avons, avecques
l'ayde de Dieu, conquesté tout le pays des Dipsodes; je te donne la chatel-
lenie de Salmigondin."

"Ha, ha. You're a fine fellow," said he. "We have, by God's help, conquered
the whole country of the Dipsodes. I confer on you the Wardenship of
Salmagundia."[2]

Thus the Rabelaisian giant's laughter does not lead to raw meat as with
crudelis Aiax, but rather to stew—*salmigondis.*

This particular type of laughter seems to be especially contagious in
Rabelais, sharing in that mysterious quality of *sympathie naturelle.* The
spirit of *compagnie* is often moistened by wine in Rabelais—" 'En sec jamais
l'ame ne habite' " (" 'The soul never dwells in a dry spot' ")[3]—and laughter
is on a par with drinking when done together, as is illustrated by Grandgousier, "beuvant et se rigoullant avecques les aultres" ("drinking and
joking with the others").[4] But this laughter is not the foolish mirth that
gurgles from wine-soaked gullets; it is rather the source and reason for
bringing out the *piot.* The first movement among the joyous companions
who receive Frère Jan is laughter, followed and still further reinforced by
drink:

Quand il feut venu, mille charesses, mille embrassemens, mille bons jours
feurent donnez:
"Hés, Frere Jean, mon amy, Frere Jean mon grand cousin, Frere Jean de
par le diable, l'accollée, mon amy!
—A moy la brasée!
—Cza, couillon, que je te esrene de force de t'acoller!"
Et Frere Jean de rigoller! Jamais homme ne feut tant courtoys ny gracieux.
"Cza, cza (dist Gargantua), une escabelle icy, auprès de moy, à ce bout.
—Je le veux bien (dist le moyne), puis qu'ainsi vous plaist. Page, de l'eau!
Boute, mon enfant, boute: elle me refraischira le faye. Baille icy que je
guargarize."

. . . and when he arrived he was greeted with a thousand caresses, a thousand
embraces, a thousand good-days:

"Ha, Friar John, my friend, Friar John, my fine cousin, Friar John, devil take you! Let me hug you round the neck, my friend."

"Let me take you in my arms!"

"Come let me grip you, my ballocky boy, till I break your back."

And what a joker Friar John was! Never was a man so charming or so gracious.

"Come, come," said Gargantua, "take a stool here beside me, at this end."

"Most willingly," said the monk, "since it is your pleasure. Page, some water! Pour it out, my boy, pour it out. It will refresh my liver. Give it here, and let me gargle."[5]

If reciprocity is quickly established between wine and laughter, the *puree Septembrale* should be seen as the outcome, and the mirth as the source in that it is preexistant and continuing. The narrator attests to the self-engendering power of laughter when he writes "c'estoit passetemps celeste les veoir ainsi se rigouller" ("it was a heavenly sport to see them thus fro-licking").[6] *Risus risum reddit,* laughter makes laughter, would be an axiomatical statement from Rabelais's comic system. Seeing and hearing hearty laughter causes laughter, even aside from the reason for such laughter. This truth is confirmed over and over in the novel from Janotus in the *Gargan-tua,* "Ensemble eulx commença rire Maistre Janotus, à qui mieulx mieulx, tant que les larmes leurs venoient es yeulx" ("Then Master Janotus began to laugh with them, and they laughed one against the other till the tears came into their eyes")[7] to Chiquanous in the *Quart Livre,* "Chiquanous rioit par compagnie." A final example can be seen toward the end of the *Quart Livre,* when, under the influence of laughter, the not-so-merry band becomes joyful once again, the weather turns for the better, and spirits are rejuvenated:

"Maniere de haulser le temps? Ne l'avons nous à soubhayt haulsé? Voyez le guabet de la hune. Voyez les siflemens des voiles. Voyez la roiddeur des estailz, des utacques et des scoutes. Nous haulsans et vidans les tasses, s'est pareillement le temps haulsé par occulte sympathie de Nature."

"How to raise good weather? But haven't we raised it, as fine as you like? Look at the wind-gauge on the scuttle. Listen to the whistling of the wind. Look how taut the stays, the ties, and the sheets are. As we raised and emptied our glasses, good weather has been raised likewise, by an occult sympathy of Nature."[8]

An awesome power seems to animate this *transfusion des espritz* that Rabelais mentions in the *Ancien Prologue,*[9] and much that is unutterable in companionship is given voice in a simple greeting extended among friends. "Ha, ha! Bien et beau s'en va Quaresme!" ("Ha, ha! Fair and softly Lent goes by!"), we recall, had become a fixed expression of salutation.[10] Indeed, it is often in such simple laughter that profound and complex feelings are expressed.

Bad Laughter

Notwithstanding, Joubert describes other kinds of laughter, and Rabelais's laughers cluster about these epithets as well. The Homeric wrath of the narrator is felt, for example, when he growls convulsively at those who attack his source of mirth in the prologue to the *Tiers Livre.* A terrible *Ris Ajacin* accompanies his lust for blood: "Estez vous encore là? Je renonce à ma part de Papimanie, se je vous happe. G22. g222. g2222. Davant davant!" ("What, are you still there? I'll renounce my share in Papimania if I can get my teeth into you. Gzz, gzzz, gzzzz!").[11]

Another laugher, in a less serious vein, yet equally vehement in his expression of the fiendish joy of the vanquisher, is Homenaz. Associating himself with and singing the praises of the unparalleled power of canon law, he crushes verbally and vicariously the *privileges de toutes Universités,* gloating in victorious laughter:

"— Ce sont, dist Homenaz, les Decretales, sans lesquelles periroient les privileges de toutes Universités. Vous me doibvez ceste là! Ha, ha, ha, ha, ha!"

"Why, the Decretals, of course," proclaimed Greatclod, "without which all the privileges of all the Universities would decay. I've taught you something there! Ha, ha, ha, ha, ha!"[12]

His emotion approaches paroxysm, his control slips momentarily: "Icy commença Homenaz rocter, peter, rire, baver et suer" ("Here Greatclod began to belch, fart, laugh, dribble, and sweat").

Although perhaps a degree lower in intensity, Dindenault's laughter is also *superbus* as he haughtily chortles Panurge: "'Han, han, qui ne vous congnoistroyt, vous feriez bien des vostres'" ("'Humph, humph! you would make a pretty ass of anyone who didn't know you!'"). Sure of his superiority, the merchant relentlessly pursues Panurge, fleering without mercy:

LE MARCH. "Fourchez là. Ha, ha, vous allez veoir le monde, vous estes le joyeulx du Roy, vous avez nom Robin mouton. Voyez ce mouton là, il a nom Robin, comme vous. Robin, Robin, Robin. — Bês, bês, bês, bês. — O la belle voix!"

DINGDONG. "Shake hands, man, there! Humph! You are touring to see the world, you are the king's fool, your name is Robin Mutton! Have a look at that sheep, there; his name is Robin just like yours. Here, Robin, Robin, Robin. Beeeeh! beeeh! beeeh! A fine voice he has, eh?"[13]

This same *mal-talant* colors each of these causes of laughter; seeing them grouped together under Joubert's epithets, while validating the terms, helps us to sense more keenly the emotions that vitalize ill-intentioned laughter and, ultimately, affords us a better understanding of the character of the laughers.

Still less energetic is the *Ris Sardonien* that seems to typify the hatchet losers in the prologue to the *Quart Livre*. The insignificant loss of a *coingnée* was reputed to bring untold wealth in return. Intentions are not guileless among the numerous dispossessed in this episode:

"Hen, hen, dirent ilz, ne tenoit il qu'à la perte d'une coingnée que riches ne feussions? Le moyen est facile et de coust bien petit. Et doncques telle est on temps present la revolution des Cieulx, la constellation des Astres et aspect des Planettes que quiconques coingnée perdera soubdain deviendra ainsi riche? Hen, hen, ha! par Dieu, coingnée, vous serez perdue, et ne vous en desplaise!"

"Ho, ho, so we only need to lose a hatchet to become rich men, do we? That's easy enough and costs very little. So the revolution of the heavens, the constellation of the firmament, and the aspect of the planets are at present such that whoever loses his hatchet will immediately become a rich man? Ho, ho, ho, my dear hatchet, you're going to get lost, if you don't mind. Lost you shall be, by God!"[14]

Such forced laughter belongs to these sneaks feigning great bereavement:

Et de crier, et de prier, et de lamenter, et invocquer Juppiter. "Ma coingnée, ma coingnée, Juppiter! Ma coingnée decza, ma coingnée delà, ma coingnée, ho, ho, ho, ho! Juppiter, ma coingnée!"

Now there was such a crying and praying and lamenting and calling on Jupiter—"My hatchet, my hatchet, Jupiter! My hatchet here, my hatchet there, oh, oh, oh, Jupiter, my hatchet!"

Forced laughter is also behind Rondibilis's *Ris canin.* He accepts Panurge's money for the consultation while his counterfeit refusal trails behind:

Puys [Panurge] s'approcha de luy et luy mist en main, sans mot dire, quatre Nobles à la rose.
Rondibilis les print tresbien, puis luy dist en effroy, comme indigné: "Hé, hé, hé, monsieur, il ne failloit rien. Grand mercy toutesfoys. De meschantes gens jamais je ne prens rien; rien jamais des gens de bien je ne refuse. Je suys tousjours à vostre commendement.
— En poyant, dist Panurge.
— Cela s'entend," respondit Rondibilis.

Then he [Panurge] went up to him and, without saying a word, put four rose nobles in his hand. Rondibilis took them most eagerly, but said with a start, as if offended: "He, he, he, my dear sir, it really wasn't necessary. Thank you all the same. From wicked people I never take anything. From honest people I never refuse anything. I am always at your service."
"So long as I pay you," said Panurge.
"That's understood," replied Rondibilis.[15]

The doctor's humor is *feint & simulé,* every bit as calculated as the carefully measured chiasmus he cleverly delivers to camouflage his venality. All are as detestable as their pursy laughter.

A general observation may be made concerning feigned laughter and genuine laughter in Rabelais. The artificial brand draws the edges of the mouth back into a frozen *rictus,* as in "hen hen," or "hé, hé, hé." The deep sincere laughter of the well-intentioned most often comes out with the back vowels, as when the giant laughs at Panurge's new way of building the walls of Paris: "Ho, ho, ha, ha, ha!"

Mad Laughter

There remains, among Joubert's epithets, causeless laughter that is nonetheless real. For the theoretician, it is an indication of *sottise,* acute or chronic. Panurge's excessive nervous reaction upon realizing that he is safe from the cosmic stir of the storm and once again within reach of *terra firma* seems to illustrate well Joubert's *Ris Catonien:* " 'Ha, ha, s'escria Panurge, tout va bien. L'oraige est passée. . . . Ha, ha, ha, par Dieu, tout va bien. . . .' " (" 'Ha, ha,' cried Panurge. 'All's well. The storm's over. . . . Ha, ha, ha, all's well, by God!' ").[16]There might even seem to be an element of victorious laughter in Panurge's outburst; indeed, we are tempted, as modern readers, to analyze it as the excess energy of his fright translated, upon sudden relief, into verbal hysterics. But in a century unaware of psychological theories of the comic, Joubert fails to see the precise cause that we would attribute to such laughter. We should not be surprised, then, when Frère Jan accuses Panurge of groundless panic: " '—Resvez tu? dist Frère Jan. Ayde icy. . . . Nostre nauf est elle encarée?' " (" 'Are you raving?' asked Friar John. 'Come here and help us. . . . Has our ship struck a reef?' "); and later, " '—Par le digne froc que je porte, dist frère Jan à Panurge, couillon mon amy, durant la tempeste tu as eu paour sans cause et sans raison' " (" 'By the worthy cloth I wear, my pusillanimous friend,' said Friar John to Panurge, 'you had no cause or reason to be frightened during the storm' "). It is easy enough for us to see Panurge's outburst here in the same light as we see his thunderous mirth of relief at the very end of the *Quart Livre;* yet for the monk, the distinction is clear between the puck's reaction to the two situations. Thus Rabelais's laughers confirm Joubert's conception of uncaused hilarity, and together they help us to understand Panurge's character as measured by his fellowmen: a coward overcome by folly in a tense situation.

Two other laughers deserve mention here, even if their status as Rabelaisian characters can be put into question. The novelist calls upon them more for reference than for a place in the plot. Philomenes and Zeuxis, whom we met in a previous analysis, both serve as examples of excessive laughter, entirely out of proportion with the causes given, and therefore, *sine re.* They substantiate both Joubert's epithet and his idea of therapeutic laughter, which normally acts as a buffer, taming extreme emotions: "Quant à mourir de tel excés, il n'et pas fort aisé: car la contraccion ampeche la prodigue dissipacion d'espris" ("As for dying from such an excess, it is not very easy: for the contraction hinders the overdissipation of spirits" [*TR,* 139–40]). Later in the treatise he is more explicit:

Et non seulemant cette affeccion nous plait, ains aussi et la plus seure de toutes: par ce qu'il n'y ha point d'extreme epanouïssemant de coeur (qui et fort dangereus) comme il avient de la grand'joye: ny vehemante constriccion, comme an la grand'tristesse.

And not only is this emotion the most pleasing to us, but also the safest of all of them: because in it there is no extreme expansion of the heart (which is very dangerous) as is the case in great joy: nor vehement constriction, as in great sorrow. (*TR,* 233)

But the laughter of Philomenes and Zeuxis is both groundless and excessive. It is exceptional, and the result is exceptional: death. Normal laughter is, by Joubert's very definition, the alternate embracing of opposite extremes. In some cases, however, *tumultueus* mirth ("*Ris Thorybode*") is fatal. Joubert, whose attention seems ever-riveted on the laugher, has an explanation for these particular cases. Not easily convinced that a healthy, normally constituted laugher would die, even from strong laughter, well-intentioned, ill-intentioned, or *Inepte,* he establishes the following hypotheses:

... Philemõ, qui paravãture avoit passé plusieurs nuïs sans dormir, & pour lors il dinoit assés tard: par ce que s'amusãt à quelque discours fort attantivemant, il ne santoit la faim, ou bien la meprisoit.

... Philomenes, who had perhaps gone several nights without sleep, and had been taking his dinner quite late, for, spending time very attentively on some speech, he did not feel his hunger, or else he paid no attention to it. (*TR*, 349–50)

Philomenes was not taking proper care of his health. Hungry and fatigued, he was able to offer no resistance to laughter when it dissipated the small amount of spirits remaining:

> le Ris demesuré dissipa le reste, aneantit ses forces, rompant le lien de son ame, ja fort extenuée an vn corps tout vsé & consumé de l'etude.

> unbounded laughter dissipated the rest of his spirits, destroyed his strength, breaking the link of his soul, which was already very extenuated in a body worn and undone by study. (*TR*, 350)

A robust and healthy man would never have died. But since, as Joubert states, philosophers are usually skinny, slight, and delicate, "*maigre, transi & delicat,*" being scarcely more than spirits, it is but a small step for them from life to death. As for Zeuxis, his age and his talent work against him, as Joubert sees it:

> Et que Zeuxis aussi fut vieus, outre que nous an lisons, il aet bien vray-semblable: d'autant que chacun se rand toujours avec le tams, plus parfait & excellant an son art. Si la grace & perfeccion de son ouvrage, luy donna occasion de rire excessivemãt, & de mourir ansamble, on peut bien conjec-turer de celà, que l'ouvrage etoit mervelheus, & le paintre fort cõsumé an son art.

> And that Zeuxis also was old, beyond what we read about it, it is very probable: so much the more in that each makes himself, with time, more perfect and excellent in his art. If the grace and perfection of his art-work gave him the occasion to laugh excessively, and withal to die, one can conjecture from it that the work was marvelous, and the painter most consummate in his art. (*TR*, 351)

Since the theoretician is so elaborate, spending several pages in possible explanations, it is obvious that he is highly motivated in bringing these cases of lethal laughter more into harmony with his general theory. The point of his argument is that death is never brought about by *le Ris*; even in these two exceptional cases, expiration is more a result of a weakness in their general condition than of one of the most admirable actions of man, "vne des plus amirables accions de l'hõme" (*TR, 6*).

Summary

The value of Joubert's treatise is not limited to its general theory, categories, and divisions of the laughable. In furnishing a list of types of laughter, it also consecrates much attention to the laugher and to his laughter as an expression of his individuality. Not only is the majority of these epithets certified by Rabelais's laughers, but the comparison of the qualifiers describing the particular types of laughter and the characters in the novel provide a means of further appreciating Rabelais's laughers.

If one applies Freud's remarks concerning dreams and personality to laughter, the following maxim results: *as they laugh, so do they be.* Laughter, intimately tuned to the individual's being, reflects that being's character throughout its modes.[17] It sings his secret nature while carefully preserving his continuing mystery.

Chapter 7

Laughter for Joubert and Rabelais

THE PUBLIC FOR WHICH Rabelais writes is not the *spectateurs* that Molière will address over a century later. It is, rather, a reading public. If we are to believe Rabelais when he writes to Monseigneur Odet, it is a public composed of laughing readers for the most part, even if some, *de mal* as the author calls them in the prologue to the *Tiers Livre,* come to incriminate his work and to *compisser* his literary wine barrel. In emphasizing the fact that the Renaissance audience was a reading one, we intend to diminish neither the theatrical qualities of Rabelais's *roman* nor the sonorous virtues of its style through which it participates fully in both the oral and the oratorical tradition. We seek merely to draw attention to the fact that we are at a time in the history of French letters characterized by a consciousness of texts and of readers of texts, of languages and of interpreters of languages. Only a few years before, François Ier had appointed the *lecteurs royaux.* Those who appreciate the obscure and obscene pages of Rabelais's freshly published work are more humanists than *mondains*; the smell of ink and the clatter of presses give way only slowly to the perfume and elegant conversation of the literary *salons* and finally to the powder and cream of the actor on Molière's stage.

Without the *truchement,* the intermediary, of the *comédien* between the eyes and ears of the public for which the *roman* was designed, Rabelais's manner of preserving the life of his comic creation must be quite different from Molière's. This is the problem we hope to clarify. Precisely what accompaniment quickens Rabelais's work? What element guarantees the crucial passage from writer to reader?

Joubertian Alternance

We must not be surprised if Rabelais does not clearly express his own comic theory anywhere in the four books, for this is not the task of a comic genius. His conception of laughter must be deduced much in the same manner as, say, Plato's esthetic theory or Freud's idea of wit.[1] Joubert's thoughts, on the other hand, are perfectly ascertainable; there is no need to interpret what he says concerning laughter.

To review very briefly, the motive force behind laughter is, in Joubert's mind, to be found in the heart where the two contrary emotions of joy and sorrow, one a manifestation of *manque de pitié,* the other of ugliness, cause contraction and dilatation. Since they are in conflict, Joubert falls naturally upon *alternance* as a means of avoiding the biological dilemma of cardiac arrest:

La raison nous apprãd que deus côtraires mouvemans ne peuvet etre fais ansãble: ains il faut que l'vn cesse auant que l'autre commance.

Reason teaches us that two contrary movements cannot be executed together: it is necessary that one cease before the other begins. (*TR,* 89)

His theory is undoubtedly a product of the Aristotelian principle of contradiction, but its application here is strictly physiological.[2] According to Joubert, laughter comes from an ambiguous state or feeling in man: "Il nait de deus contraires, desquels l'vn ampesche l'autre d'etre excessif" ("It is born of two contraries, one of which hinders the other from being excessive" [*TR,* 87]). A marginal note indicates that the engendering emotion is not simple but mixed: "Il faut bien que l'affeccion soit double ou melee, tout ainsi que son obiet" ("It is necessary that the emotion be double or mixed, just as is its object" [*TR*, 87]). Laughing matter, therefore, in the Renaissance theorist's eyes, is by definition ambiguous.

Yet if man is actually to laugh over the numberless ambiguities he perceives, be they in word or in deed, only the temporal solution of alternance will allow mirth's actualization:

> Nous avons declaré tout ce qui precede l'acte du Ris: c'et la matiere ridicule, portee au coeur . . . lequel emù d'icelle, et agité alternativemāt de contraires & soudains mouvemās.

> We have declared all that precedes the act of laughter: it is the laughable material, carried to the heart . . . which is moved by this material, and alternatively churned by sudden and contrary movements. (*TR*, 90)

This is because the law of contradiction is as implacable on the physical level as it is on the spiritual. Just as a proposition cannot be, at the same time, both affirmed and denied, analogously, two opposite actions cannot take place at the same time in the same place. Joubert expresses this simple physical truth both in Latin and in French: "*Nemo potest simul flare & sorbere* . . . car on ne peut souffler ou expirer, & susser tout ansamble" ("no one is able to inhale and exhale at the same time" [*TR*, 122]). No movement takes place if two equal opposite actions seek actualization simultaneously.

Alternance, then, is the law by which finite reality marks its own progression and extension in time and space.[3] Joubert, probably recalling Ficino, reiterates for those of his own time the idea that laughter, a sort of microcosmic alternance, shares in the enduring harmony of the macrocosm,[4] thus preserving man from death, as long as *ridicula* lasts: "autāt que dure la matiere du Ris, soit dit, soit fait, soit pansee, ainsi le rire cōtinue" ("as long as the laughable matter lasts, either in word, in act, or in thought, so long will the laughter last" [*TR*, 89]). In what sense, however, can this notion apply to Rabelais's work?

Rabelaisian Alternance: Texture of the Laughable Text

In the preceding chapters we have seen that Rabelais's work provides its own laughing matter by providing its own laughers. Although they establish the tone and the comic value of many of the commonplaces that appear in the four books, they do not reveal the structural anatomy, the physiological characteristics of the work. We are referring here to particular traits or perhaps a major recurrent one that may be traced anatomically, so to speak, throughout the organism of the *roman,* constituting the principle of its stylistic behavior. Joubert's theory suggests such a motif.

Hugues Salel's *dizain*[5] portrays Rabelais as a "Democrite / Riant les faictz de nostre vie humaine" ("Democritus / Mocking the deeds done in the life of man").[6] With this epithet comes the invitation to turn our attention once again to this ancient Greek philosopher who was unable to stop laughing at his vision of a universe composed entirely of atoms in constant clash, movement, and hustle and bustle.

The Birth of a Giant: Its Sustenance and Continuation

Gargantua's contrary emotions as witnessed at the birth of Pantagruel the giant lead one to meditate upon the native structural qualities of *Pantagruel* the book. Rabelais's recourse to the figures of antithesis and commutatio is particularly evident in the opening paragraph of chapter III:

> Quand Pantagruel fut né, qui fut bien esbahy et perplex? Ce fut Gargantua son pere. Car, voyant d'un cousté sa femme Badebec morte, et de l'aultre son fils Pantagruel né tant beau et grand, ne sçavoit que dire ny que faire, et le doubte que troubloit son entendement estoit assavoir s'il devoit plorer pour le dueil de sa femme, ou rire pour la joye de son fils. . . .

> When Pantagruel was born, who do you think was really amazed and perplexed? Gargantua, his father. For seeing, on the one hand, his wife Badebec dead, and on the other hand, his son Pantagruel born, so handsome and so big, he did not know what to say or do. The doubt which troubled his mind was whether he should weep over the death of his wife or laugh over the birth of his son. . . .[7]

These figures can be seen here as representing very appropriately the contrary states of life and death, but at the same time they indicate the fertile interplay of these opposites in the mind of the writer as they generate a portion of the text. The particular variation on the general leitmotiv used in the opening sentence is that of question-answer: " . . . qui fut bien esbahy et perplex? Ce fut Gargantua son pere." The mechanism of Rabelaisian composition is thus prefigured, since it is later seen to animate the entire paragraph.

Long before arriving at the third chapter of *Pantagruel,* however, the reader encounters already in the prologue to *Gargantua* another facet of this double direction in thought. Floyd Gray has pointed out the fundamental ambiguity riding not only the prologue, but the entire work as well.[8] The *Gargantua*'s poetics are thus also prefigured in the prologue's invitation-disinvitation. Gérard Defaux has called attention in a well-documented article to the preponderance in the four books of clear-cut oppositions. He also affirms that the main theme of Rabelais's entire masterpiece is the comparison between Socrates and the *silenes,* made up of a constant interplay of oppositions and antitheses.[9] Indeed, even earlier in Rabelais's work this filing of opposites is encountered. With the opening words of the prologue is witnessed the stepping up and down between two levels of discourse: "Beuveurs tresillustres . . . Verolez tresprecieux." ("Most illustrious drinkers . . . most precious syphilitics.").[10] Adjectives such as *tresillustres* and *tresprecieux* belong to a noble and bookish style, whereas *Beuveurs* and *Verolez* are immediately perceived as more coarse and associated with the spoken language.

Other examples at the sentence and subsentence level of this participation in high and low style may be seen in many of the names that Rabelais invents:

les seigneurs de Baisecul et Humevesne
saint Pansart
saint Balletrou
soeur fessu
les colonelz Riflandouille et Tailleboudin
le Duc de Francrepas
le Comte de Mouillevent
le Seigneur de Painensac

the lords of Kissmyarse and Suckfizzle
Saint Fatpaunch
Saint Bunghole
Sister Buttocky

the Colonels Maul-chitterling and Chop-sausage
the Duke of Freemeal
the Earl of Wetwind
the Lord of Bread-in-bag[11]

The concept of polar interplay is fundamental in these "noble" or "holy" characters' names.

If we move up to the level of longer and more complex sentences, the basic pattern takes on variations: the device becomes the handmaid of art in the sense that it makes what is not so appear to be so. The simple pendular phases of the cardinal principle of alternance begin to change slightly, taking on modifications:

> Les ungs mouroient sans parler, les aultres parloient sans mourir. Les ungs mouroient en parlant, les aultres parloient en mourant.

> Some died without speaking, others spoke without dying. Some died in speaking, others spoke in dying.[12]

Alternance, here used to express the idea of ubiquitous death, is equally effective in conveying the impression of the repetitious cycles of physiological life. The author begins to weave nuances with his binary oppositions:

> ... c'est assavoir à boyre, manger et dormir; à manger, dormir et boyre; à dormir, boire et manger.

> ... that is, in drinking, eating, and sleeping; in eating, sleeping, and drinking; in sleeping, drinking, and eating.[13]

Analysis reveals the formula: Rabelais assigns to the first term of each new infinitival threesome the second term of its predecessor. The mechanism makes a complete cycle in that its ending would engage perfectly into its beginning, making for an eternal tumbling system in miniature. But the artifice of this microcosm of words is so well disguised that only the heartbeat, the elementary *taedium* of biological continuity, strikes the reader's consciousness.

It is the heart of the reader that senses even more keenly this alternance when it takes place on the paragraph level. It is well known that in 1534 the *Gargantua* preceded the *Pantagruel,* which had most probably been published two years earlier.[14] What is important is that even in the prologue to *Pantagruel,* the first moments, so to speak, in the life of Rabelais's creation, the paragraphs are made to participate in this *balancement* between two emotional fields. In speaking of the *Grandes et inestimables Cronicques* to which he will soon compare his own masterpiece, the author entreats the reader to put aside troubles and daily toil to pursue and peruse—to use a metathesis not uncharacteristic of Rabelais—his work:

> Et à la miẽne volunte q̃ ung chascũ laissast sa ppre besoigne & mist ses affaires ppres en oubli / affin de y vacquer entierement sans q̃ son esprit feust de ailleurs distraict ny empeche . . . car il y a plus de fruict que par-adventure ne pensent ung tas de gros talvassiers tous croustelevez / qui entendent beaucoup moins en ces petites ioyeusetez que ne faict Raclet en Linstitute.

> It is my wish that every reader lay aside what he has to do, . . . forget all about his own affairs, in order to concentrate his attention exclusively . . . his mind neither distracted nor elsewhere. . . . For there is greater profit in them than a motley lot of poxed critics would have you believe, who understand these little drolleries even less than Rachet the *Institutes.*[15]

The paragraph itself passes from sadness to joy as it enjoins the reader to put aside the mind's distress under life's oppressive routine to contemplate wholly the soothing and amusing stories awaiting him.

This same motif is used in the paragraph immediately following. He begins with the hunters who become sad as they see their efforts at venery fall short of the fleeting fowl:

> s'il advenoit que la beste ne feust rencontrée par les brisées ou que la beste se mist à planer, voyant la proye gaigner à tire d'esle, ilz estoient bien marrys, comme entendez assez.

> if it so happened that the animal was not tracked down or that the falcon refused to soar in pursuit, they were most irritated, as is quite natural, when they saw their prey escaping.[16]

But consolation is no further off than the nearest copy of the *Grandes chronicques.* The joy of reading these gigantic and *inestimables faictz* saves the huntsmen from the great hurt of failure:

> mais leur refuge de reconfort, et affin de ne soy morfondre, estoit à recoler les inestimables faictz dudict Gargantua.

> but they found refuge and comfort, and a way out of their exasperation by rereading the inestimable exploits of said Gargantua.

Needless to say, the reader is made to undergo the to and fro motion of these extremes as he continues his reading.

Ensuing paragraphs are cast in similar fashion. Alcofribas reminds us of the medieval *marchand des quatre saisons* (huckster) barking out the miraculous qualities of his merchandise. The particular variation of the general schema here is pain-relief. Toothache is remedied by mere application of said *Chroniques.* Next come the suffering syphilitics. The paragraph begins with a description of their pain:

> O, quantes foys nous les avons veu, à l'heure que ilz estoyent bien oingtz et engressez à poinct, et le visaige leur reluysoit comme la claveure d'un charnier, et les dentz leur tressailloyent comme font les marchettes d'un clavier d'orgues ou d'espinette quand on joue dessus, et que le gosier leur escumoit comme à un verrat que les vaultres ont aculé entre les toilles!

> How often have we seen them covered with ointment and grease, their faces glistening like a larder keyhole, their teeth chattering in their heads like an organ or spinet keyboard when it is played upon, and their throats foaming like a boar's at bay when chased by a pack of bloodhounds into a net!

The transition from the suffering to the relief is abrupt: one brief question (*Que faisoyent-ilz alors?*) marks the sensation barrier. The rest of the paragraph treats their soothing:

> Que faisoyent-ilz alors? Toute leur consolation n'estoit que de ouyr lire quelques page dudict livre, et en avons veu qui se donnoyent à cent pipes de vieulx diables en cas que ilz n'eussent senty allegement manifeste à la lecture dudict livre, lorsqu'on les tenoit es lymbes, ny plus ny moins que les femmes estans en mal d'enfant quand on leurs leist la vie de saincte Marguerite.

What did they do then? Their sole consolation was to have someone read to them a few pages from said book. And I have seen some who would give themselves to five score giant casks of devils if they did not obtain manifest relief from the reading of this book while they were being held in limbo, in much the same way as women in childbirth do when someone reads to them from the *Life of St. Margaret*.

These one-two movements between opposites seem to constitute the basic schematism of the author's pen.

Raymond Lebègue felt the lifelike quality of Rabelais's metronomic rhythms, so apt in portraying the progression of physiological reality in time.[17] The tail of Gargantua's *jument* levels all the trees of Beauce:

A tort, à travers, de çà, de là, par cy, par là, de long, de large, dessus, dessoubs, abatoit boys comme un fauscheur faict d'herbes, en sorte que depuis n'y eut ne boys ne freslons, mais feust tout le pays reduict en campaigne.

Crossways and lengthways, here and there, this way and that, to front and to side, over and under, she swept down the trees as a mower does the grass, so that since that time there has been neither wood nor hornets, and the whole country has been reduced to a plain.[18]

But this rhythm of alternates, if we come back now to the scene of Pantagruel's birth and Badebec's death, is felt to reign at the paragraph level and even beyond. The reader, as he pursues his *lecture,* takes part in what Jean Paris calls its basic structure: l'*alternance.* [19] Made by Rabelais to travel across these contrary emotional fields, the reader participates in what might be called the comic rhythm according to Joubert's conception of laughter. After the introductory paragraph announcing the principal motif, the entire chapter is a constant *va-et-vient* of paragraphs shifting between the two moods of joy and sorrow: " 'Pleureroy-je? disoit-il. Ouy, car pourquoy? Ma tant bonne femme est morte' " (" 'Shall I weep?' he cried. 'Yes, but why? Because my dear sweet wife is dead' ").[20] Answer follows question as Gargantua exhibits at length his lamentable state. He registers no less than a dozen complaints, the last of which characterizes adequately the tone of the preceding eleven jeremiads:

"Ha, faulce mort, tant tu me es malivole, tant tu me es oultrageuse, de me tollir celle à laquelle immortalité appartenoit de droict!"

"Ah, false death, how evil, how outrageous thou art to have taken from me one to whom immortality rightly belonged!"

Although the depth of his sadness can be doubted as he enumerates in a rhetorically windy strain the reasons that justify his weeping, the giant's *dueil* is clearly the cause of his sorrow: "Et, ce disant, pleuroit comme une vache" ("And, as he spoke, he cried like a cow").

His laughter, on the other hand, is associated with the joy taken in the idea of his newborn son. Again, no transition marks the passage of emotions. The movement is more than hearty; it is stark: "Mais tout soudain rioit comme un veau, quand Pantagruel luy venoit en memoire" ("But suddenly, remembering Pantagruel, he laughed like a calf"). The next paragraph depicts the unspeakable joy of the giant father over his infant son:

"Ho, mon petit filz (disoit-il), mon coillon, mon peton, que tu es joly, et tant je suis tenu à Dieu de ce qu'il m'a donné un si beau filz, tant joyeux, tant riant, tant joly. Ho, ho, ho, ho, que suis ayse! Beuvons, ho! laissons toute melancholie! Apporte du meilleur, rince les verres, boute la nappe, chasse ces chiens, souffle ce feu, allume la chandelle, ferme ceste porte, taille ces souppes, envoye ces pauvres, baille leur ce qu'ilz demandent! Tiens ma robbe, que je me mette en pourpoint pour mieulx festoyer les commeres."

"Ha, my little son," he said, "my ball, my fartlet, what a fine fellow you are. How endebted I am to God who has given me such a handsome son, so gay, so happy, so fine! Ho, ho, ho, ho, how happy I am! Let's drink! Ho! let us put aside all sorrow! Bring out the best wine, rinse the glasses, set the table, drive out the dogs, poke up the fire, light the candles, close the door, slice the bread for the soup, send away these poor, give them anything they ask for. Hold my doublet. Let me put it on so as to be ready to receive the ladies."

It is not necessary to reproduce here the entire chapter; the above passages expose clearly enough the Rabelaisian motif. Jean Paris reveals this same schematism on a more developed scale. He perceives a preponderant antithetical movement wheeling its way through the *Gargantua*: "Tout le livre, en effet, apparaît réductible à douze séquences de variable longueur, où comique et sérieux s'éclipsent tour à tour" ("The whole book, as a matter of fact, appears reducible to twelve sequences of varying length, in which the comic and the serious eclipse each other turn by turn").[21] He points out other systems of correspondence governed by binary symmetry.

Although one might wonder whether this vision of Rabelais's four books suggests accurately their bristle, still other critics attest to Rabelais's singular style as being the result of opposing forces in conflict, of *atomes* in constant collision. Pierre Villey, in his *Marot et Rabelais,* attributes the author's creative powers to the "mixture of very disparate elements entering into his composition, or shock of diverse and often contradictory currents which cross each other in him."[22] This sensitive critic shows that in spite of the great differences that exist between the first two books and the *Tiers Livre,* the fundamental characteristic is its double presentation: "the art of his composition consists in developing both sides of the subject, the popular side and the learned side."[23]

It is hardly necessary to demonstrate that the third book differs considerably from *Pantagruel* and *Gargantua* in many aspects. Rabelais's twelve-year silence intervenes, and one must expect considerable changes after an author lifts his pen for over a decade, particularly when the turbulence following the Affaire des Placards (1534) invades such a pause. The loose sequence of interrupted chronological development that characterizes the sporadic unfolding of the birth, education, and exploits of the hulking giants is no longer the dominant logical thread. We see nothing of the fabulous adventures promised in the last chapter of *Pantagruel.* The fabric of adventures gives way to the fabric of dissertations and consultations.[24]

Yet a profound comic periodicity persists. For all the changes observed in the novel's appearance, its ambiguity is still felt. Villey pinpoints it as "the mixture of the familiar and the severe that constitutes the characteristic form of gaiety of the *Tiers Livre.*" He also reduces Rabelaisian humor to saying amusing things gravely and grave things amusingly.[25] The change in the work's conduct seems to lie in the liberation of a lyric force upsetting both time and the elements in the opening chapters of the third book. Much like the unchaining of the demon that Rabelais refers to in the third chapter, Panurge's eulogy upsets the pacing progression of the first two books:

"Lucifer se desliera, et sortant du profond d'enfer avecques les Furies, les Poines, et Diables cornuz, vouldra deniger des cieulx tous les dieux. . . ."

"Lucifer will break his bonds and, issuing from the depths of hell with the Furies, fiends, and horned devils, will try to dislodge the gods of all nations, major and minor alike, from the heavens. . . .[26]

The giants give way to Panurge; Rabelais's work will now owe its movement and continuation to a man-size giant. Nevertheless, only the poles are reversed, for the basic leitmotiv of alternance remains. It is as though an imaginary mirror were placed after the first two books, offering an inverted reflection-projection of the *Tiers* and *Quart Livre*. This seems to be the vision that Villey suggests of the reflective silence that cleaves the work, making of it an opposing twain:

In the *Tiers Livre*, along with the seriousness of ideas, the austerity of an intemperate erudition mixes with the banter. The relationship of the contrasting elements is reversed: and contrary to *Pantagruel*, one is tempted to say here that the learned matter constitutes the essential, and that Rabelais colors it in a popular manner, either by the tone of the exposition, or by the ends to which he applies this matter.[27]

Thus the metered movement of the giants becomes internalized but is still felt. The alternance passes to the level of ideas, represented by characters or places, but the essential *drame* continues.

Michel Beaujour, equally intrigued by Rabelais's use of opposition in the *Tiers* and *Quart Livre*, mentions that the characters are not *balzaciens*, but are set up in an oppositional interplay to permit what Northrop Frye calls the genre of anatomy:

. . . a form of prose fiction, traditionally known as the Menippean or Verronian satire and represented by Burton's *Anatomy of Melancholy*, characterized by a great variety of subject-matter and a strong interest in ideas. In shorter form it often has a *cena* or symposium setting and verse interludes.[28]

The great French critic Albert Thibaudet compares the *Tiers Livre* to Plato's

Symposium. Marcel Tetel adds the following commentary to this fertile parallel: "... in the *Tiers Livre* as well as in Plato's work there is this to and fro of argumentations presenting the pro and contra of a question. The comic particular to the *Tiers Livre* is a sort of global comic which springs from a juxtaposition of scenes in which diverse characters express contradictory ideas."[29] Pantagruel and Panurge, of course, form the most evident contrasting couple. Yet each consultation becomes a moment of alternation for Panurge himself: he changes with liquid facility from his role of pursuing the issue to that of avoiding it. When Raminagrobis composes a poem made up entirely of oxymora, its form resembles too closely the very nature of Panurge. Seeing his impossible situation, he flees himself. His contrasting roles are internal and therefore ambiguous: he is a living paradox. He assumes the part he does not have and has the part he would not assume. The final touch of ambiguity enters and takes full possession when one tries to decide which Panurge is *persona* and which is *figura.* From a systematic and docile searcher, Panurge switches to an irrational reactionary, refusing to accept the true image of his own foolish quest and of his own irrational self. Anger or fear accompany his moods of violence. Later, when the ambiguity of Trouillogan's answers depicts only too clearly the same double nature of Panurge himself, the same vehemence explodes in blasphemy and cursing:

> "Or ça, de par Dieu, j'aymeroys par le fardeau de sainct Christofle, autant entreprendre tirer un pet d'un asne mort que de vous une resolution. ...."
> "Par la chair, je renie; par le sang, je renague; par le corps, je renonce. Il m'eschappe."

> "Come now, in Heaven's name! By the burden of Saint Christopher, I'd as soon undertake to get a fart out of a dead donkey as an answer out of you. ...."
> "God's flesh, I give it up! God's blood, I throw in my hand! God's body, I abjure! He's slipping out of my grasp."[30]

Eternally *mobile,* Panurge can seize neither himself nor that which imitates him.[31]

If internal alternance is the more general trait in the *Tiers Livre,* there are remnants of the external oxymora that were more frequent in *Gargantua* and *Pantagruel.* Here Panurge speaks of the gift of sleep invaded by troubling dreams and abrupt awakenings in paradoxical terms:

> "tel don en fascherie et indignation ne peut estre terminé sans grande
> infelicité praetendue. Aultrement seroit repous non repous, don non don,
> non des dieux amis provenent, mais des diables ennemis, jouxte le mot
> vulgaire, *echthron adora dora.*"

> "such a gift cannot end in anger and irritation without some great misfor-
> tune being portended. Otherwise rest would not be rest and a gift would not
> be a gift, since it would not come from the gods, our friends, but from the
> devils, our enemies. Remember the common proverb: *the presents of enemies
> are not presents.*"[32]

The structure matches Panurge's dialectics. We have only to turn the page
for an example of an entire paragraph built upon antitheses. The Rabelaisian pace seems tireless as it covers here night and day, work and play:

> "Nature a faict le jour pour soy exercer, pour travailler, et vacquer chascun
> en sa neguociation; et pour ce plus aptement faire, elle nous fournist de
> chandelle, c'est la claire et joyeuse lumiere du soleil. Au soir elle commence
> nous la tollir et nous dict tacitement: 'Enfans vous estez gens de bien. C'est
> assez travaillé. La nuyct vient: il convient cesser du labeur et soy restaurer par
> bon pain, bon vin, bonnes viandes; puys soy quelque peu esbaudir, coucher
> et reposer, pour au lendemain estre frays et alaigres au labeur comme dav-
> ant.'"

> "Nature made the day for exercise, for work, and for each man to occupy
> himself in his business; and to help us do this more deftly, she provides us
> with a candle, the clear and joyful light of the sun. In the evening she begins
> to withdraw it from us, as much as to say to us: 'You are good honest
> children. That's enough work. Night is coming, and now you ought to cease
> from your labours and take some refreshment. What you need is good bread,
> good wine, and good meat. After that you should enjoy yourselves a bit,
> then lie down and rest, so as to be fresh and joyful for your next day's
> labours.'"

Even the binomial rhythm felt while reading the paragraph on the giant's
jument in the *Gargantua* is maintained in the *Tiers Livre*. The reader is con-

stantly rocked as he pursues the enjoyable work of progressing through Rabelais's chapters. Here is another instance in which characters' emotions are divided into two opposed fields:

Comment Pantagruel et Panurge diversement
exposent les vers de la Sibylle de Panzoust

CHAPITRE XVIII

Les feueilles recuillies, retournerent Epistemon et Panurge en la Court de Pantagruel, part joyeux, part faschez. Joyeulx, pour le retour; faschez pour le travail du chemin, lequel trouverent raboteux, pierreux et mal ordonné.

Pantagruel and Panurge find different explanations
for the Verses of the Sibyl of Panzoust

CHAPTER XVIII

When they had collected the leaves, Epistemon and Panurge returned to Pantagruel's court, partly glad and partly vexed; glad at their return, but vexed by the labours of the road, which they found rugged, stony, and ill-made.[33]

Among the endless churning of Latin maxims interspersed with the text throughout the Bridoie episode, there is one that should retain our attention as particularly representative of the recurring complexities of the legalistic world, and that recalls at the same time the Rabelaisian mixture: "*Interpone tuis interdum gaudia curis*" ("Intersperse your sorrow with joy").[34] The texture of the *Tiers Livre* is, as Barbara Bowen has recently concluded, one of ambiguity, paradox, even folly.[35] Even if twelve years of silence on the author's part cause these characteristics to internalize, and to mature, both internal and external alternance still mark the work's movement and its makeup. It seems to course.

The *Quart Livre*, last of the unquestionably authentic books of the *roman*, is found to resemble its predecessors in this respect. Beginning with the *abios bios, bios abiotos* oxymoron of the prologue, antithetical phrases, sentences, paragraphs, and entire chapters are juxtaposed. Ambiguity also continues to be present. Alfred Glauser sensed what Joubert lets us see clearly concerning this aspect of the work when he comments on the willful

ambiguity established on *l'isle Ennasin* as it inevitably leads to laughter.[36]
Juxtaposing the *Papefigues* and the *Papimanes* is also typical of Rabelais's
style. As Barbara Bowen has said, such an artifice suggests that "they are
two halves of the same picture, when in fact they are not remotely connected."[37] Such switching of parts is what animates the social gathering
sponsored by a neighbor of the seigneur de Guyercharois. The ladies of the
village disguised the pages "en damoyselles bien pimpantes et atourées"
("as fair and attractive young women"). The ambiguity caused error and
error, laughter:

> "Les paiges endamoysellez à luy entrant près le pont leviz se presenterent. Il
> les baisa tous en grande courtoisie et reverences magnifiques. Sur la fin, les
> dames, qui l'attendoient en la guallerie, s'esclatterent de rire. . . ."

> "and when he arrived these petticoated pages were waiting for him beside the
> drawbridge. He kissed them all most courteously, with a magnificent bow
> for each. But when he had done, the ladies who were waiting for him in the
> gallery burst out laughing."[38]

A striking example of the violent reversal of moods naked of any transition other than a new chapter heading is seen in the *Quart Livre* between
chapters XXVIII and XXIX:

> Pantagruel, ce propous finy, resta en silence et profonde contemplation.
> Peu de temps après, nous veismes les larmes decouller de ses oeilz grosses
> comme oeufz de austruche. Je me donne à Dieu, si j'en mens d'un seul mot.

> *Comment Pantagruel passa l'isle de Tapinois, en laquelle*
> *regnoit Quaresmeprenant*

> ### CHAPITRE XXIX

> Les naufz du joyeulx convoy refaictes et reparées, les victuailles refraischiz,
> les Macraeons plus que contens et satisfaictz de la despense que y avoit faict
> Pantagruel, nos gens plus joyeulx que de coustume, au jour subsequent feut
> voile faicte au serain et delicieux Aguyon, en grande alaigresse.

> When Pantagruel had finished his story he remained silent, in a profound
> meditation. A little while afterwards we saw the tears rolling down from his
> eyes, as big as ostrich eggs. God take my soul, if every word I say isn't the
> truth.

Pantagruel sails past Sneaks' Island,
where King Lent used to reign

CHAPTER XXIX

When the ships of the jovial company were refitted and repaired, and their victuals had been replenished, the Macreons were left thoroughly satisfied and contented with Pantagruel's expenditure on their island. Our men, too, were more jovial than usual when we set sail on the following day, in high spirits, with a sweet and pleasant wind behind us.[39]

Pantagruel's grief is instantly dispersed by the joy of departure as the band prepares to leave the *isles des Macraeons.*

Major and minor characters also continue to represent opposite camps. Roles are reversed so frequently on *l'isle d'Ennasin* that they are finally lost completely. The resulting ambiguity invites Renaissance laughter:

Leurs parentez et alliances estoient de façon bien estrange; car, estans ainsi tous parens et alliez l'un de l'aultre, nous trouvasmes que persone d'eulx n'estoit pere ne mere, frere ne soeur, oncle ne tante, cousin ne nepveu, gendre ne bruz, parrain ne marraine de l'autre. Sinon vrayement un grand vieillard enasé, lequel, comme je veidz, appella une petite fille aagée de trois ou quatre ans: mon pere; la petite fillette le appelloit: ma fille.

Their relationships and degrees of kinship were of a very strange kind. For they were all so related and intermarried with one another that we found none of them who was a mother or a father, a brother or a sister, an uncle or an aunt, a cousin or a nephew, a son-in-law or a daughter-in-law, a god-father or a god-mother, to any other; except indeed for one tall noseless old man, whom I heard calling a little girl of three or four, Father, while the little girl called him, Daughter.[40]

This chapter where *d'estranges alliances* are discussed is possible only because of associated opposing couples. Jean Plattard made special note of this fact in speaking of these minor characters: "Rabelais's entire invention consists in personifying each term of the substantive couples and in assuming kinship relations between these individuals."[41] Likewise, each major character seems to have an inversed correlative whose nature and interests are diametrically opposite. At the beginning of chapter XVIII, for example, upon seeing the monks on their way to the council of *Chesil,* "Panurge entra en excès de joye," but Pantagruel "restoit tout pensif et melancholique" ("Panurge was overjoyed"; Pantagruel "stood by, pensive and melancholy"). [42]

Still other oppositions occur. The storm scene brings about a veritable polarization between Frère Jan and Panurge. The monk speaks on behalf of the intrepid sailors and Panurge, alone, represents the side of the fear-stricken *pleurart:*

"— Dieu, dist Panurge, et la benoiste Vierge soient avec nous! Holos, holas! Je naye. Bebebebous, bebe, bous, bous. *In manus.* Vray Dieu, envoye moy quelque daulphin pour me saulver en terre comme un beau petit Arion. Je sonneray bien de la harpe, si elle n'est desmanchée.

"— Je me donne à tous les Diables, dist frere Jan (Dieu soit avecques nous, disoyt Panurge entre les dens), si je descens de là, je te monstreray par evidence que tes couillons pendent au cul d'un veau coquart, cornard, escorné. Mgnan, mgnan, mgnan! Vien icy nous aider, grand veau pleurart, de par trente millions de Diables qui te saultent au corps! Viendras tu ô veau marin? Fy, qu'il est laid le pleurart!"

"God and the blessed Virgin be with us," wailed Panurge. "Alas, alas, I'm drowning. Bebebebous, bebe, bous, bous. Into Thy Hands! Dear God, send me a dolphin to carry me ashore like a sweet little Arion. I shall play my harp most beautifully, if it's not ruined."

"All the devils may take me," said Friar John. "God be with us," muttered Panurge between his teeth. "But if I come down there to you," resumed Friar John, "I'll give you good proof that your balls hang from the arse of a cuckoldy calf, a horned calf with a broken horn. Mgnan, mgnan, mgnan. Come here and help us, you great weeping calf, in the name of thirty thousand devils. May they leap on your body! Are you coming sea-calf? What an ugly blubberer he is!" [43]

Fear is pitted against boldness, and Frère Jan's cursing alternates with Panurge's soft-spoken reparative prayers. The principle of literary creation here, as elsewhere in Rabelais is, to use Plattard's expression, simple but fecund. [44]

Although conceiving of Rabelais's entire work as an exercise in alternance might seem unwarrantable, the perceptual experience that one has of the text in time (reading) complements and sustains this overview. The mind finds easy the manipulation of antitheses, gross oppositions, and alternance. As Albert-Marie Schmidt has stated so well, "the human mind, by an inherent laziness, likes violent, rapid, and false contrasts; it takes delight in opposing God and the devil, good and evil, the sun and the moon, and day and night."[45]

Rabelais understood this truth and puts into practice the art of composing an entire literary cosmos of such seemingly facile mechanisms of dramatic conflicts. Although all of the ideas, concepts, or currents traveling in this intricate network of basically simple components may be difficult or impossible to explicate today, it is obvious that the author's principal concern is in a simple, forceful, exaggerated and even falsified representation of the great problems, complexities, and ambiguities popular among his readers. His recourse to alternance and opposition was fruitful in arousing the reader's pleasure, insuring his diversion and well-being, if we are to trust Rabelais's own words concerning the success of his novel:

> Vous estez deuement adverty, Prince tresillustre, de quants grands personaiges j'ay esté et suis journellement stipulé, requis et importuné pour la continuation des mythologies Pantagruelicques: alleguans que plusieurs gens languoureux, malades, ou autrement faschez et desolez, avoient, à la lecture d'icelles, trompé leurs ennuictz, temps joyeusement passé, et repceu alaigresse et consolation nouvelle. Es quelz je suis coustumier de respondre que, icelles par esbat composant, ne pretendois gloire ne louange aulcune; seulement avois esguard et intention par escript donner ce peu de soulaigement que povois es affligez et malades absens, lequel voluntiers, quand besoing est, je fays es presens qui soy aident de mon art et service.

> You are well aware, most illustrious Prince, how many great personages have been, and daily are, pressing me, urging me, and begging me for a continuation of the Pantagrueline fictions. They tell me that many dispirited, sick, and otherwise moping and sadly persons have escaped from their troubles for a cheerful hour or two, regained their spirits and taken fresh consolation by reading them. My usual answer is that I composed them for my own amusement, and have claimed no praise or glory for them; that my sole aim and purpose in writing them down was to give such little relief as I could to the sick and unhappy, in my absence, as I gladly do when with them in their moments of need, and when my art and services are requested.[46]

Rabelais's playground undoubtedly astounded many of its contemporaries, as Marcel De Grève has convincingly argued.[47] It is true, as Pierre Jourda has emphasized, that Rabelais did not write for the drinking and syphilitic commoners.[48] Yet nothing hinders the *beuveurs tresillustres* and the *verolez tresprecieux* from being humanists of prodigious erudition. We must not fail to recall that Erasmus, the great humanist *par excellence,* fits at least into the latter group, if not the former.[49]

The reading of Rabelais's novel is enhanced by a knowledge of Joubert's treatise on laughter because it affords us not only some precise examples and categories of sixteenth-century humor, but also additional insight into the ideology shared by the people of the time as well as by the characters in the novel. The antithetical commonplace of the microcosm in the macrocosm can be applied to the work itself: from the "atoms" of Democritus to the literary cosmos itself, the molecular prefigures the universe.[50] The microcosm of literal word-in-play heralds the macrocosm of world-in-play, each individual constituent forming a living image of the whole, the whole being an inspiring image for each individual part. A similar idea is tersely expressed by the philologist Joseph Scaliger in a chiasmus under Joubert's likeness on the treatise's frontispiece:

Ce livre de Ioubert,	Et toute la Nature,
Ha exprimé l'image	Ha exprimé l'image
De toute la Nature:	De ce maeme Ioubert.
This book of Joubert's	And all Nature
Has expressed the image	Has expressed the image
Of all Nature	Of this same Joubert.

Man's book expresses the image of the world, and the world expresses the image of man. The epigraph could be applied to theoretician and novelist alike. Rabelais's work, by its endless interplay of opposites,[51] imitates the movements of the laugher as Joubert anatomizes them.

Alfred Glauser has anatomized critically the poetics of Rabelais's act of composition when he likens it to a feverish fencing. Such a comparison is quite close to the idea of a vigorously physical sport, bordering on the dangerous: "if style (*stilus*) is the point which writes, it can be imagined in him as the movements of a foil; his whole being is involved in the act of writing, an invisible fencing takes form in his work, an enchanted movement in which an entire world acts, strikes, leaps, and dances."[52] One is reminded of the *sikinnis* to which Rabelais himself seems to allude in the prologue to the *Quart Livre:*

> A ces motz, tous les venerables Dieulx et Deesses s'eclaterent de rire, comme un microcosme de mouches. Vulcan, avec sa jambe torte, en feist pour l'amour de s'amye, trois ou quatre beau petitz saulx en plate forme.

> At these words all the venerable gods and goddesses burst out laughing, like a microcosm of flies, and Vulcan with his twisted leg performed three or four little jigs on the dais, for the love of his mistress.[53]

It is this movement of the *sikinnis,* the dance performed by the satyrs in the ancient Greek plays, that is felt to animate Rabelais's style. This dance, more a series of leaps than a sequence of steps, was a vehement and hurried pace recalling a rhythmed running or skipping—a sort of laughter translated into the dance form. The relationship between the reader and the book, the communication in which this curious texture is sensed, ultimately breathes life into this *chant alterné,* this *blason alterné,* that characterizes for Glauser Rabelais's literary creation.[54] The act of reading furnishes the pulse as it is pursued across the successive doubles presented ceaselessly by the author's pen. How this movement actually comes to be perceived by the reader is a notion that Jean-Paul Sartre considers in *Qu'est-ce que la littérature?:*

> For the literary object is a strange spinning-top which exists only in movement. To make it rise, a concrete act is necessary which is called reading, and it lasts only as long as the reading is able to last.[55]

In Rabelais's case, we know that this *lecture* is able to continue as long as the laughing matter supports the laughing reader, and vice versa, as Joubert indicates: "autant que dure la matiere du Ris, soit dit, soit fait, soit pansee, ainsi le rire cõtinue" ("as long as the laughable matter lasts, either in word, in act, or in thought, so long will the laughter last" [*TR,* 89]).

But laughing matter is ambiguous, as the theorist reminds us: "Il faut bien que l'affeccion soit double ou melée, tout ainsi que son obiet" ("It is necessary that the emotion be double or mixed, just as is its object" [*TR,*

87]). This is precisely the element that Floyd Gray has underscored in speaking of the Prologues as prefigurations of an entire work of which the nature is ambiguous.[56] Trying to decide, therefore, when Rabelais is or is not serious on the basis of dangerous allusions in his work, as several critics have done, is not likely to reveal its *vis comica* in the sixteenth century.[57] The entire work should be all the more comic, all the more exhilarating, *because* it is ambiguous. This is the direction that Joubert's theory indicates, at least for the laughers of the time.

Both theorist and practitioner state the idea that too much joy or sorrow is detrimental to man's well-being. If the young Renaissance experienced excessive joy, sadness seemed to be the dominant trait that Rabelais read on the features of his compatriots when he wrote his *dizain:* "Voyant le dueil qui vous mine et consomme" ("When I see grief consume and rot / You").[58] An ambiguous synthesis was the answer; a restless quintessence resembling man himself might restore him to his natural state, a solution involving the sigh, but which would break it, interrupt it, and make it take on the movement and the breath of life: a sort of vital mixture.

Summary

Insofar as Rabelais uses alternance and closely related structures and figures of antithesis, ambiguity, and paradox as a means of literary creation, his choice of a creative technique corresponds to Joubert's with the difference that Joubert uses the motif in the area of thought and Rabelais, more in language. Their means of resolving their respective difficulties of creation and explanation (Rabelais's practice and Joubert's theory) is alternance. They are therefore as closely related as theory can be informed by practice. Joubert will never explain the myriads of Rabelaisian laughter, nor will his categories capture sufficiently the innumerable devices at work—often in concert—in a single episode of the *roman;* yet in much the same way as Aristotle seizes Aeschylus's vitality, Boileau Racine's, and Bergson Molière's, Joubert leads us to the heart of Rabelaisian mirth. Without drawing so much as one example from the four books, the theoretician invites us to unveil their vital principle of laughter.

To the degree that Rabelais's work imitates man, representing him in his confused state, alternating as does the giant father Gargantua from one emotional extreme to the other, to the extent that the book itself as a work of art appears to be more human than bookish, appearing or attempting to be what it is not or what it can never really be, it is fulfilling one of the laws of the comic as observed by Joubert. The book imitates the microcosm that is man. In this respect Rabelais's work is in itself comic by antithetical standards of the time. It is essentially comic not only because of the laughable matter that it contains but because what it does is laughable: it mimics what it is not. It is as though the limits of humanity break down at the traditional limits of man's epidermis, letting that which characterizes *homo ludens* pass into and inhabit Rabelais's book. The work of art may thus become almost as human as man himself. The book imitates nature, in this case the human nature of laughing man, and this imitation, this *mimesis,* makes the work comic not only in content, but in its structural behavior.

Conclusions

AT A TIME IN THE HISTORY of France when man's heart was anxious and divided in constant political and religious issues, when the conflicting evidence and emotions over new discoveries perplexed and confused several generations, Joubert was writing his theory of laughter. The very subject of his investigation was one that made sense of the ambivalence felt by himself and his fellow laughers. As Rabelais exhorted his reader to put aside his mental business and troubles ("Et à la mienne volunté que chascun laissast sa propre besoigne, ne se souciast de son mestier et mist ses affaires propres en oubly"), claiming that man's natural state was laughter ("Pour ce que rire est le propre de l'homme"), so, too, Joubert expressed the same philosophy at the beginning of the last book of his *Traité:*

> Or la vertu & puissance de rire, et à bon droit peculieremant, concedee à l'home, afin qu'il eut moyen de recreer quelquefois son esprit, travelhé & lassé d'occupacions serieuses, comme de l'etude, contamplacions, composicions, traité d'affaires, administracions publiques, & samblables propres à l'homme. Car de tous les animaus le seul homme et né apte à l'etude, contamplacion, negociacion, & toute sorte d'affaires, laiquelles occupacions le randet vn peu rude, severe, chagrin, difficile, brusque, facheus & melancholique.

> Now the virtue and power of laughter is rightly conceded to man especially, so that he might have the means to recreate at times his mind, worked and fatigued by serious occupations, such as study, contemplation, composition, commercial concerns, public administration, and others common to man. For of all the animals only man is born capable of study, contemplation, negotiation, and all sorts of activities, which occupations make him a bit rough, severe, sad, difficult, brusque, angry, and melancholy. (*TR,* 231–32)

Joubert shared with Rabelais the belief that man was made by the Creator to be both social and happy, and that laughter was a divine gift destined to make man more human, happy, and sociable:

> Et d'autant qu'il convenoit à l'homme d'etre animal sociable, politic & gracieus, afin que l'vn vequit & coversat avecques l'autre plaisammant & beninemant, Dieu luy ha ordonné le Ris, pour recreacion parmy ses de-

portemans: afin de lacher quelque fois comodemant les reines de son esprit: . . .

And insomuch as it is fitting for man to be a sociable, political, and charming animal, in order that one might live and converse with the other pleasantly and benignantly, God has ordained laughter for him as a recreation
among his activities, to conveniently loosen at times the reins of his
mind. . . .(*TR,* 232)

But laughter for both Joubert and Rabelais involved more than simple joy.
Its precise function is more elegantly illustrated when the theoretician
compares it to the gift of wine, likewise bestowed upon mankind to assist
him in accepting the hard fact of old age and, eventually, ultimate negation
in death. Its role was that of being a mediator, as is that of laughter:

. . . tout ainsi qu'il ha donné le vin aus hommes, pour tramper & adoucir la
severité & austerité de la vielhesse, comme disoit Platon, etant cette liqueur
moyenne, & la plus tamperee de tous les sucs qui peuvet nourrir l'homme.
Aussi le Ris nous et tresagreable de ce que il retient certaine mediocrité antre
toutes ses affecciõs.

. . . in just the same way that He has given wine to man, to dilute and
lighten the severeness and austereness of old age, as Plato used to say, since
this liquid is moderate, and the most tempered of all the juices which can
nourish man. Laughter also is most gratifying in that it retains a certain
balance between our emotions. (*TR,* 232–33)

Readers of Rabelais recall immediately the novelist's own definition of
Pantagruelisme: "c'est certaine gayeté d'esprit conficte en mepris des choses
fortuites" ("a certain gaiety of spirit produced by a contempt of the inci-
dentals of fate"), as well as his praise of *mediocrité:* "Mediocrité a esté par les
saiges anciens dicte aurée, c'est à dire precieuse, de tous louée, en tous en-
droitcz agréable" ("The ancients held that moderation was golden, that is
to say precious, universally praised and everywhere welcome").[1]
Joubert then describes, within the confines of his theory, what it is about
laughter that soothes the heart of man in a most efficacious way:

Et non seulemant cette affeccion nous plait, ains aussi et la plus seure de
toutes: par ce qu'il n'y ha point d'extreme epanouïssemant de coeur (qui et

fort dangereus) comme il avient de la grand'joye: ny vehemante constriccion, comme an la grand'tristesse.

And not only is this emotion the most pleasing to us, but also the safest of all of them: because in it there is no extreme expansion of the heart (which is very dangerous) as is the case in great joy: nor vehement constriction, as in great sorrow. (*TR,* 233)

Aristotle, whom both doctors endorsed, believed the heart was the center and source of life and feeling in man. Any injury to its normal systole-diastole action might well be heavy with consequences. Those who suffer the strains of extreme emotion are indeed closer to death than they would suppose: "plusieurs de petit courage, se pamet aisémant de joye, ou de tristesse, & quelques vns an meuret" ("many who are of small heart, faint easily from joy or from sorrow"). Laughter, on the other hand, in the manner of a most wise alchemist, blends the respective violence of the acid and the alkaline in man's soul, neutralizing conflicts that would threaten severely his well-being: "mais on ne lit pas que beaucoup de jans soint mors de rire" ("but one does not read that many people die of laughter" [*TR,* 233]).

The nature of laughter is difficult to seize; this truth was announced by Joubert at the threshold of his treatise. Being a Christian, he sought through syncretism to reconcile the nature of man as fashioned by God with that same nature as observed by Aristotle and his mentors and successors:

le Createur ha ainsi formé nottre ame, que antre plusieurs autres facultés, elle ha pouvoir & aptitude au Ris. Et c'et (je panse) ce que diset les Philosophes, que la puissance de rire depand de la forme de l'homme, & qu'elle et cachee an son ame, ou qu'elle influe d'icelle immediatemant: comme nous disons communemant des proprietés de quelque chose.

the Creator has so formed our soul that among several faculties, it has the power and ability to laugh. And this (I think) is what the Philosophers say, that the power to laugh depends on man's nature, and that it is hidden in his soul, or that it flows directly from it: as we say commonly that a thing's properties do. (*TR,* 235)

The power to laugh lies in man's soul, but for Joubert, the act of laughter has its source in the heart of the *microcosme.* The common human acts, those

that seem the simplest, are often those to which the Creator assigns complex and enormous tasks such as regenerating, maintaining, and soothing
man in his *continuation:* "sa majesté vse le plus souvant de l'ordinaire" ("His
majesty uses most often the ordinary"). Laughter answers for all that man
alone cannot solve. Its voice is as defiant as the challenge thrown in man's
teeth by the awesome greatness of a continuing cosmos: "haulteur, profon-
dité, longitude, et latitude" ("height, depth, length and breadth").[2]
Thomas M. Greene in his work on Rabelais's comic courage notes well the
truth of hilarity's worth as a rampart during the perplexing moments of
life. Joubert himself, deeper in theory than the novelist, called upon laughter in the throes of the ever-thickening difficulties that surrounded him in
the study of this most mysterious of subjects:

> Toutesfois la difficulté ne nous doit aucunemant retirer de l'antreprise, ains
> plutost nous exciter & hausser le courage, nous souvenans du vieus proverbe,
> *Les choses difficiles sont les belles,* ou autremant, *les belles sont difficiles.* Aussi y
> sommes nous angagés de nottre promesse faite au precedāt livre, ayans
> promis de traiter cette question, laquelle vient icy mieus à propos.

> Nevertheless, the difficulty must in nowise make us withdraw from the
> enterprise, but rather excite and heighten our courage, as we remember the
> old proverb, *Difficult things are the beautiful ones,* or, *the beautiful ones are
> difficult.* We are also committed to do it by our promise in the preceding
> book, having promised to treat this question, which now happens to be more
> apropos. (*TR,* 190)

A play on words seems to bolster his courage and restore his resilience. Yet
with this very thought, still another question clouds the theoretician's
mind: is it the wordplay that fires the laughter or unquenchable laughter
that engenders the laughable?

Throughout the foregoing chapters, we have seen Rabelais's laughers
illustrate Joubert's observations on the laughable. Although in a few occurrences, incidents in the novel that fit into Joubert's categories do not
provoke laughter, in these very cases, the context of the particular situation
corresponds exactly to his explanations for lack of laughter in certain emotionally charged circumstances. Yet the closer the theoretician approaches
the cause of laughter logically, the more the internal stability of the investigation falters. The logic of the treatise breaks down when we examine the

physiological sieve (the senses) that Joubert uses to sift laughable *fais &*
propos, "deeds and words." Curiously enough, this very discrepancy points
the way to Rabelais's *ridicula.*

In spite of such difficulties, Joubert finishes his task. His final words,
those of a scholar, close fittingly his voluminous treatise:

> I'ay achevé an ces trois livres, la principale histoire du Ris, & tout ce qui
> m'et venu à l'esprit jussqu'à presant, touchant cette matiere. Si desormais je
> rancontre an ravassant, autre chose de cet argument, j'an transferay vn quat-
> rieme. Ce pendant je prie aus lecteurs, qui ont la grace de mieus philosopher,
> ne vouloir dedaigner cette besogne: ains y amployer quelque peu de leur
> industrie, pour l'anrichir de leurs plus doctes & solides raisons.

FIN

> I have completed in these three books the principal history of laughter,
> and all that has come to mind up to the present concerning the subject. If in
> the future, upon thinking on it, I happen across other things for the argu-
> ment, I shall transfer them in a fourth book. In the meantime, I beg those
> readers who have the ability to philosophize better than I, not to disdain this
> work, but to employ their industry a bit in enriching it with their learned
> and solid justifications.

END   (TR, 352)

Joubert's fortitude in his inquiry amidst unstable terms and swaying
categories produced a work that enables us to throw new light on Rabelais's
incomprehensible mirth. Rather than correcting social unbalance with satire, which, as Bergson contends, is the primary function of laughter in the
nineteenth century, Rabelais seeks to remedy internal instability. Much
more in keeping with the older meaning of *satire,* a mixture, Rabelais
alternates his moods and levels of discourse to insure the work's therapeutic
effect, which, during the medically oriented Renaissance period, is not to
be seen as radically separated from its esthetic effect.[3] What is good for
man's personal well-being, physically and spiritually, is beautiful. In this
sense, Rabelais's enterprise has a profound esthetic direction. The
etymological sense of the word is closer to this interpretation: *aisthanomai,*
"I perceive," or "I feel." Rabelais leads us to beauty and truth through a

profoundly human form that emanates from his work: it is none other than laughter. Just as the form of the *palimpseste* marks, in Gérard Genette's mind, the whole of Proust's creation,[4] it must be stated that Rabelais's work is constantly inspired by its own laughter.

But laughter is not able to exist unless there are mixed feelings over something. This is the conclusion that Joubert invites us to draw, and that Rabelais forces us to accept. Arthur Koestler's explanation of the comic (bisociation theory) is undoubtedly the most satisfying for us as modern readers, since our educational tradition favors psychological explanations.[5] Yet this theory would not have found fertile soil to receive it in sixteenth-century France; the intellectual arena was medicine, and the dust raised was over physiological theories.[6] Fertile parallels can be drawn between the two theories, but our purpose has lain elsewhere. Due to the attention given in the field of modern psychology to unresolved conflict, our notions of ambivalent feelings and contrary emotions have come to be pejorative. Far from being viewed as sources for laughter, they are undesirable, presenting in varying degrees eventual problems for the individual. During the Renaissance, however, such "problems," dilemmas, enigmatic realities, paradoxes, and ambiguities are the fountainhead of mirth, as stated in Joubert's treatise and as constantly borne out in Rabelais's comic practice. M. A. Screech is correct when he writes that Rabelais is not always comic, but his remarks apply to our laughter.[7] Joubert's conception allows the phenomenon of Renaissance laughter to embrace the whole of Rabelais's work.

Comical literature, as a genre, depends ultimately upon its readers' laughter, and in speaking of Renaissance literature we must draw a conclusion similar to Rosalie Colie's concerning paradox: "Paradox requires a beholder willing to share in its action and by thus sharing in it to prolong that action."[8] Rabelais's novel provides such beholders in creating for itself laughing readers. But whereas paradox is intellectual and remains relegated to the cerebral sphere, laughter continues toward externalization. What was previously internal alternance, internal ambivalence, internal tension of a spiritual nature, is transferred to the emotional level. At this stage, as Joubert carefully explains, it generates the convulsion we know as hearty laughter. It is a physiological manifestation of the human incapacity to resolve opposites. Man may admit this failure in several ways, one of which is to withdraw and whimper. But the laugher is one who shouts over and through the failure victoriously. Renaissance laughter is therefore paradox made flesh; its life continues in the laughing reader. Floyd Gray has spoken similarly of the reader's role:

> But if he [the reader] accepts the book as Rabelais offers it, that is, as a substantial draught from his creative barrel, then he will appreciate its multiple aspects, its various directions, he will prolong its creative movement without arresting it in a conclusion.[9]

In reexamining our findings, we see that, with only a few exceptions, every category drawn by Joubert is gorged with Rabelaisian laughter. Not only do the four books contain incidents that we might think hilarious, but they also provide laughers to confirm their comic value at the time. Joubert's epithets of laughter also show that Rabelais's characters are seen—and heard—to permeate every type of laughter that the Renaissance theoretician imagined. The presence of laughter in Rabelais is, therefore, apparent; its abundance by sixteenth-century standards is undeniable.

Joubert will never do justice to Rabelais's boisterous mirth, but he does keep the modern reader from the pitfall of saying that *since* Rabelais's book is full of ambiguity it was *therefore* not comic. On the contrary, our study of the *Traité du Ris* demonstrates that because Rabelais's work is ambiguous, drawn with contradictions, sewn with paradox, and stitched with antitheses, it had every chance to arouse laughter in the sixteenth century. It is perhaps the incomprehensible breadth of this mirth that inspired Victor Hugo's vision of Rabelais and his laughter as godlike. This divine fatherhood is felt in Hugo's lines as the *auctor divinus* soothes the first of the laughing animals:

> Rabelais, que nul ne comprit:
> Il berce Adam pour qu'il s'endorme,
> Et son éclat de rire énorme
> Est un des gouffres de l'esprit.
>
> Rabelais, whom no one has understood:
> He rocks Adam so that he may fall asleep,
> And his enormous burst of laughter
> Is one of the gulfs of the mind.

It is only after reading Joubert that it makes sense to claim that Rabelais's work is not only overflowing with laughers and laughing matter, but that it actually is *laughing matter*. *L'oeuvre rit,* as Glauser so often suggests. The entire book is, organically, constantly undergoing the convulsions, the heavings, the alternating resolutions and recrudescences of forces that characterize laughter as it is conceived of by Joubert. Rabelais's work is, then, in this sense, laughing matter possessed by a *daimon;* it is a comical domain truly animated by the lifebreath of its laughing subjects, be they narrators, characters, readers, or the work's own mimicry of man in the throes of Joubertian mirth. Rabelais's comic creation is the only one of its kind in French literature—perhaps in any literature—to breathe forth its own humor, and therefore its own life, ambiguity, and mystery. It does this internally, externally, thematically, and stylistically, through its laughers and by its laughter.

Notes

Introduction

1. *Rabelais: La Vie très horrificque du grand Gargantua,* Chronology and foreword by V.-L. Saulnier; introduction and glossary by Jean-Yves Pouilloux (Paris: Garnier-Flammarion, 1968), p. 16.

2. Marcel De Grève, *L'Interprétation de Rabelais au XVIe siècle* (Geneva: Droz, 1961), p. 60.

3. This article is in *François Rabelais: Ouvrage publié pour le quatrième centenaire de sa mort 1553-1953* (Geneva: Droz, 1953), pp. 74-85. The Affaire des Placards was the violent aftermath of a particular event in Protestant opposition to the Mass. When in 1534 inflammatory posters were fixed to the king's bedchamber door, the royal reaction was severe: François Ier had several Protestants burned or hanged.

4. Lucien Febvre, *Le Problème de l'incroyance au XVIe siècle: La Religion de Rabelais* (Paris: Albin Michel, 1942; rpt. 1968), pp. 424-28.

5. M. A. Screech, *Aspects of Rabelais's Christian Comedy,* Inaugural lecture (London: H. K. Lewis, 1968), p. 15. Other works by Screech dealing wholly or in part with the comic are: *The Rabelaisian Marriage: Aspects of Rabelais' Religion, Ethics & Comic Philosophy* (London: E. Arnold, 1958); *L'Evangélisme de Rabelais* (Geneva: Droz, 1959); "The Legal Comedy of Rabelais in the *Tiers Livre* of *Pantagruel,*" in *ER* 5: 175-95; "Aspects du rôle de la médecine dans la philosophie comique de Rabelais," in *Invention et Imitation: Etudes sur la littérature du seizième siècle* (The Hague and Brussels: Van Goor Zonen, 1968), pp. 39-48; and in collaboration with Ruth Calder, "Some Renaissance Attitudes to Laughter," in *Humanism in France,* ed. A. H. T. Levi (London: Manchester University Press, 1970), pp. 216-28.

6. Raymond Lebègue, "Rabelais et la parodie," *BHR* 14: 193-204. Marcel Tetel's principal study on the subject was preceded by three articles: "La Tautologie chez Rabelais," *Le Français Moderne* 31: 292-95; "Aspects du comique dans les images de Rabelais," *L'Esprit Créateur* 3: 51-56; "La Valeur des accumulations verbales chez Rabelais," *RR* 53: 96-104. Another article stressing the illogic in Rabelais is by Abraham C. Keller, "Absurd and Absurdity in Rabelais," *KRQ* 19: 149-57.

7. Michel Butor, "Le Rire de Rabelais: Le Fruit d'une conquête," *Les Nouvelles Littéraires,* no. 1805.

8. Barbara Bowen, "Rabelais and the Comedy of the Spoken Word," *MLR* 63: 575-80.

9. G. J. Brault, "The Comic Design of Rabelais's *Pantagruel,*" *SP* 65: 140-46.

10. Jean Paris, *Rabelais au futur* (Paris: Seuil, 1970), pp. 223-24.

11. Leo Spitzer, "Rabelais et les 'rabelaisants,'" *SFr* 4: 401-23; Raymond Lebègue, *Rabelais* (Tubingen: Max Niemeyer Verlag, 1952); Henri Peyre, *The Liter-*

ature of France (Englewood Cliffs: Prentice-Hall, 1966), p. 28. See also the posthumous article of Spitzer, "Ancora sul prologo al primo libro del 'Gargantua' di Rabelais," *SFr* 27: 423–34. Spitzer first spoke of cosmic laughter and the mythical comic of Rabelais in his doctoral dissertation, *Die Wortbildung als stilistisches Mittel, exemplifiziert an Rabelais* (Halle: Max Niemeyer, 1910).

12. Thomas M. Greene, *Rabelais: A Study in Comic Courage* (Englewood Cliffs: Prentice-Hall, 1970), pp. 60–63, 114–15.

13. Charles Hertrich, *Le Rire de Rabelais et le sourire de son pantagruélisme* (Paris: Flambeaux, 1942), cited in V.-L. Saulnier's article, "Dix années d'études sur Rabelais (1939–1948)," *BHR* 11: 104–28. Ronald de Carvalho, *Rabelais et le rire de la Renaissance* (Paris: Emile Hazan, n. d.). See also Dr. P. E. P. Serre's thesis, "Essai d'une étude psycho-pathologique de certains types comiques dans l'oeuvre de Rabelais" (Bordeaux, 1921), and especially the biographical study by Mary P. Willcocks, *The Laughing Philosopher, Being a Life of François Rabelais* (London: Allen & Unwin, 1950).

14. Mikhail Bakhtin, *Rabelais and His World,* trans. H. Iswolsky (Cambridge: M. I. T. Press, 1968). Michel Butor and Denis Hollier have applauded Bakhtin's attempt to reemphasize the popular culture aspect of Rabelais's work in a book they coauthored, *Rabelais, ou c'était pour rire* (Paris: Larousse, 1972), p. 142.

15. Paul Stapfer, *Rabelais, sa personne, son génie, son oeuvre* (Paris: A. Colin, 1889); Jean Plattard, *L'Oeuvre de Rabelais (Sources, Invention et Composition)* (Paris: Champion, 1910); Pierre Villey, *Marot et Rabelais* (Paris: Champion, 1923).

16. *Traité du Ris, contenant son essance, ses cavses et ses mervelheus effais, curieusemant recerchés, raisonnés & observés,* By M. Laur. Ioubert. . . . Paris, Nicolas Chesneav, rue S. Iaques, at the Green Oak, M. D. LXXIX.

17. Jean Plattard, *La Vie de François Rabelais* (Paris: Van Oest, 1928), translated by Louis P. Roche as *The Life of François Rabelais* (London: Frank Cass, 1930), p. 99; Bakhtin, *Rabelais and His World,* p. 68. De Grève also mentions briefly the treatise (*L'Interprétation,* p. 178), and Lazare Sainéan speaks of Joubert's *Erreurs populaires,* but not his *Traité du Ris,* in *L'Influence et la réputation de Rabelais* (Paris: J. Gamber, 1930), p. 220.

18. "Some Renaissance Attitudes to Laughter." Strangely enough, Screech and Calder express surprise over Joubert's reticence with regard to Rabelais. This is perhaps more easily understood when one remembers Joubert's Protestant leanings, along with the fact that at the time that he was composing his *Traité du Ris,* the "responsables de Genève," as De Grève reminds us, considered Rabelais's work "meschant" and "profane" (*L'Interprétation,* p. 217).

19. Louis Dulieu, "Laurent Joubert, chancelier de Montpellier," *BHR* 31: 139–67. A complete list of Joubert's works is in this article.

20. P. J. Amoreux, *Notice historique et bibliographique sur la vie et les ouvrages de L. Joubert* (Montpellier: J.-G. Tournel, 1814). See also E. Wickersheimer's article in

La médecine et les médecins en France à l'époque de la Renaissance (Paris, 1905): "Un brave homme et un bon livre: Laurent Joubert et les *Erreurs populaires....*"

21. Screech and Calder. The most exhaustive study on Renaissance comic theory is Marvin T. Herrick's *Comic Theory in the Sixteenth Century* (Urbana: University of Illinois Press, 1964). Although this study is helpful as a point of comparison outside of France, its preoccupation with English and Italian theorists, and with practical ramifications in the theater, diminish its usefulness for us. One of its great merits is to underscore the persistence of ancient theories, particularly that of Terence, in Renaissance dramatic theory.

22. See Claire Pfenniger's "Le Rire au seizième siècle: Etude sur la nature de l'humour chez Bonaventure des Periers, Noel du Fail, Marguerite de Navarre, Jacques Yver" (Ph. D. diss., University of California, Los Angeles, 1970).

23. *JLC*, p. 216.

24. *TUPM*, p. 161.

25. *TUPM*, p. 166.

26. Febvre, *Le Problème de l'incroyance,* p. 146.

27. The still unresolved problem of the authorship of the *Cinquième Livre* necessarily excludes it from our consideration in the present study. For a recent reevaluation of the fifth book, see George Petrossian, "The Problem of Authenticity of the *Cinquiesme Livre de Pantagruel:* A Quantitative Study" (Ph. D. diss., University of Michigan, 1974), and Alfred Glauser, *Le Faux Rabelais ou l'inauthenticité du Cinquième Livre* (Paris: Nizet, 1975).

28. *Dictionnaire de la langue française du seizième siècle,* ed. E. Huguet (Paris: E. Champion, 1925 to 1967). See Barbara Bowen's comments in the section entitled "Problems of Comprehension" in the first chapter of her book, *The Age of Bluff: Paradox and Ambiguity in Rabelais and Montaigne* (Urbana: University of Illinois Press, 1972), pp. 7–17.

29. Charles Marty-Laveaux, *La Langue de la Pléiade,* vol. 2 (1886–98; rpt. Geneva: Slatkine Reprints, n. d.), pp. 9–10.

30. *JLC,* p. 664.

Chapter One

1. M. A. Screech admits his acceptance of the Bergsonian explanation in his article "Aspects du rôle de la médecine dans la philosophie comique de Rabelais," in *Invention et Imitation: Etudes sur la littérature du seizième siècle* (The Hague and Brussels: Van Goor Zonen, 1968), pp. 39–40; Barbara Bowen, in *The Age of Bluff: Paradox and Ambiguity in Rabelais and Montaigne* (Urbana: University of Illinois Press, 1972), p. 97, attributes to Tetel a distinction that Henri Bergson expressed—word for word—in *Le Rire: Essai sur la signification du comique,* 273rd ed. (Paris: P.U.F., 1969); Marcel Tetel's *Etude sur le comique de Rabelais* (Firenze:

Olschki, 1966) is clearly supported by principles and categories from Bergson, as Floyd Gray has pointed out in reviewing the study in *Symposium* 3: 81–91.

2. Lane Cooper, *An Aristotelian Theory of Comedy* (Oxford: Blackwell, 1922), pp. 162–65, 224–89. Marvin T. Herrick, *Comic Theory in the Sixteenth Century* (Urbana: University of Illinois Press, 1964), p. 44. Jean Plattard uses this traditional distinction as follows: "1. Comique de mots. . . . 2. Comique de situation" [*L'Oeuvre de Rabelais (Sources, Invention et Composition)* (Paris: Champion, 1910)].

3. Cf. Bergson, "Mais il faut distinguer entre le comique que le langage exprime, et celui que le langage crée." *Le Rire*, p. 79.

4. An important article on the use of contraries is D. W. Wilson's "Contraries in 16th Century Scientific Writing," in *Essays Presented to C. M. Girdlestone* (London: University of Durham, 1960), pp. 351–68.

5. *OCJ*, I, 76; trans. *FG*, p. 28.

6. The pertinent reference from Paré's *Introduction* is in Huguet's *Dictionnaire de la langue française du seizième siècle*, ed. E. Huguet (Paris: E. Champion, 1925 to 1967): "Risible."

7. Lucien Febvre, *Le Problème de l'incroyance au XVIe siècle: La Religion de Rabelais* (Paris: Albin Michel, 1942; rpt. 1968), p. 380.

8. M. A. Screech and Ruth Calder, "Some Renaissance Attitudes to Laughter," in *Humanism in France,* ed. A. H. T. Levi (London: Manchester University Press, 1970), p. 224.

9. Herrick, *Comic Theory,* p. 50.

10. Screech and Calder briefly discuss laughter as morally acceptable or reproachable in the sixteenth century. Although they arrive at no definite conclusion, the question is of importance and might help to explain why a number of theorists do not follow the path their arguments tend to indicate. See Paul Oskar Kristeller, *Renaissance Thought: The Classic, Scholastic, and Humanistic Strains,* rev. and enlarged ed. (New York: Harper Torchbooks, 1955; 1961).

11. Joubert is referring here to Jean Fernel. See Febvre, *Le Problème de l'incroyance,* pp. 174–79. Other *physiciens* are Jean Dubois, Pierre Tolet de Lyon, and Jean Manardi (Jean Plattard, *La Vie de François Rabelais* [Paris: Van Oest, 1928], p. 250).

12. Febvre, *Le Problème de l'incroyance,* p. 357. See also E. Callot, *La Renaissance des sciences de la vie au XVIe siècle* (Paris: P.U.F., 1951), and Paul Delaunay, "Rabelais physicien," in *François Rabelais: Ouvrage publié pour le quatrième centenaire de sa mort 1553–1953* (Geneva: Droz, 1953), pp. 36–44.

13. *De Risu libellus,* (Paris: J. Richer, 1587). See also Screech and Calder, "Some Renaissance Attitudes to Laughter." Cf. the conceptions developed during and after French Classicism: Will G. Moore, "The French Notion of the Comic," *Yale French Studies,* no. 23 ("Humor"): 47–53.

Chapter Two

1. Both Michelet in the nineteenth century and J. Delumeau of our own times were struck by the frequency of contradictions that riddle the sixteenth century. See also D. Ménager, *Introduction à la vie littéraire au XVIe siècle* (Paris: Bordas, 1968), p. 5, and Michel Foucault's remarks in *Les Mots et les choses* (Paris: Gallimard, 1966), ch. I.

2. *OCJ*, I, 9; II, 18; I, 297; II, 18; I, 304. Translations, respectively, *JLC*, pp. 6, 222, 499, and *JMC*, p. 442.

3. *OCJ*, I, 294; trans. *JLC*, p. 221.

4. *OCJ*, I, 50; trans. *FG*, p. 17.

5. See Michel Beaujour's psychoanalytic treatment of this scene, *Le Jeu de Rabelais* (Paris: L'Herne, 1969), pp. 72–73.

6. Henri Clouzot defends them with the following note in the Lefranc edition: "Ce trait de moeurs domestiques n'est pas une invention de Rabelais. On le trouve dans le *Roman de la Rose*, v. 7229, éd. elzév., t. II, p. 186:

> Sovent voi neis ces norrices,
> Dont maintes sont baudes et nices,
> Quent lor enfant lavent et beignent,
> Si les (les couilles) nomment-el autrement.

A la fin du XVIe siècle, le jeune Louis XIII n'était pas élevé autrement que Gargantua. Cf. Franklin, *Vie d'autrefois. L'Enfant*. Appendice, d'après le *Journal* d'Héroard" (*OCL*, I, 120, n. 68).

7. K. J. Dover, *Aristophanic Comedy* (Berkeley and Los Angeles: University of California Press, 1972), p. 239.

8. *OCJ*, I, 473; trans. based upon *JLC*, p. 355, and *JMC*, p. 334.

9. *OCJ*, I, 3; trans. *FG*, p. 1.

10. *OCJ*, I, 312; trans. *JMC*, p. 229.

11. Henri Bergson, *Le Rire: Essai sur la signification du comique*, 273rd ed. (Paris: P.U.F., 1969), p. 3; *Comedy: "Laughter" Henri Bergson*, ed. Wylie Sypher (Garden City: Doubleday, 1956), p. 63.

12. M. A. Screech and Ruth Calder, "Some Renaissance Attitudes to Laughter," in *Humanism in France*, ed. A. H. T. Levi (London: Manchester University Press, 1970), p. 221.

13. *L'Art Poétique*, Chant III, vv. 401–2. "The comic, enemy of sighs and tears, / Admits in its verse no tragic sorrows."

14. This is a notion that Thomas Hobbes develops much more thoroughly.

15. *OCJ*, 333–34; trans. *JMC*, pp. 243–44.

16. *OCJ*, 334; trans. *JMC*, p. 244.

17. *OCJ*, II, 231; trans. *JMC*, p. 585.

18. *OCJ*, II, 80; trans. *JMC*, p. 482.

19. It is not our intention here to draw parallels between the fictitious episode and the disputes over papal authority to which it alludes. For more historical detail, see Robert Marichal, "René du Puy et les Chicanous," *BHR* 11: 136. See also *OCL*, VI, 162–205.

20. This and the following passages from this episode are from *OCJ*, II, 69–80, and the corresponding translations are from *JMC*, pp. 475–87.

21. Jean Plattard, *L'Oeuvre de Rabelais* (*Sources, Invention et Composition*) (Paris: Champion, 1910), pp. 311, 315, 327–29; Linton C. Stevens, "Rabelais and Aristophanes," *SP* 55: 29; Marcel Tetel, *Etude sur le comique de Rabelais* (Firenze: Olschki, 1966), pp. 20–23, 83–84.

22. Mikhail Bakhtin, *Rabelais and His World,* trans. H. Iswolsky (Cambridge: M. I. T. Press, 1968), ch. 4.

23. Cf. Screech and Calder, "Some Renaissance Attitudes to Laughter," pp. 222–23.

24. The passages in this section are from *OCJ*, I, 21; II, 236; I, 403. Translations are from *JMC*, pp. 48, 287, and 588.

25. *OCJ*, I, 169; trans. *JMC*, p. 137.

26. This and the following two passages are from *OCJ*, II, 248; trans. *JMC*, pp. 596–97.

27. *OCJ*, I, 305; trans. *JMC*, p. 225.

28. *OCJ*, I, 501; trans. *JMC*, p. 353.

29. *OCJ*, II, 247; trans. *JMC*, p. 596.

30. Joubert's example is based upon a special kind of antithesis that Marvin T. Herrick calls *anteisagoge* (*Comic Theory in the Sixteenth Century* [Urbana: University of Illinois Press, 1964]), p. 195.

31. *OCJ*, I, 76; trans. *JMC*, p. 79.

32. A. J. Krailsheimer, *Rabelais and the Franciscans* (Oxford: Clarendon Press, 1963), p. 210.

33. See Screech and Calder in "Some Renaissance Attitudes to Laughter" for their remarks on Janotus (pp. 222–23). See also and especially Gérard Defaux's article, "Rabelais et les cloches de Notre Dame," *ER* 11: 1–28, and his book, *Pantagruel et les Sophistes: Contribution à l'histoire de l'humanisme chrétien au XVIe siècle* (La Haye: Martinus Nijhoff, 1973), for the intellectual history behind this episode.

Chapter Three

1. Henri Bergson, *Le Rire: Essai sur la signification du comique,* 273rd ed. (Paris: P. U. F., 1969), p. 25. For a detailed discussion of the concept of imitation as it

relates to poetry, see G. Castor, *Pléiade Poetics: A Study in Sixteenth-Century Thought and Terminology* (Cambridge: University Press, 1964).

2. See D. W. Wilson's article, "Contraries in 16th Century Scientific Writing," in *Essays Presented to C. M. Girdlestone* (London: University of Durham, 1960).

3. *OCJ*, I, 306; trans. *JMC*, p. 225.

4. *OCJ*, I, 5; trans. *FG*, p. 2.

5. See François Rigolot's article, "Rabelais et l'éloge paradoxal," *KRQ* 18: 191–98.

6. *OCJ*, II, 91; trans. *JMC*, p. 489.

7. The meaning that A. J. Greimas gives to the term *grimuche* is "figure grotesque." *Dictionnaire de l'ancien français jusqu'au milieu du XIVe siècle* (Paris: Larousse, 1969), p. 323.

8. *OCJ*, I, 103; trans. *FG*, p. 46.

9. N. C. Carpenter, *Rabelais and Music* (Chapel Hill: University of North Carolina Press, 1954), p. 15.

10. Alfred Glauser, *Rabelais créateur* (Paris: Nizet, 1966), p. 27. Our translation.

11. Further discussion of this subject is in Zevedei Barbu's book, *Problems of Historical Psychology* (London and New York: Routledge and Kegan Paul and Grove Press, 1960).

12. On this aspect of Panurge, see Paul Stapfer, *Rabelais, sa personne, son génie, son oeuvre* (Paris: A. Colin, 1889), p. 386; Georges Lote, *La Vie et l'oeuvre de François Rabelais* (Paris: Droz, 1938), p. 368; Glauser, *Rabelais créateur*, pp. 131–69. See especially Ludwig Schrader's study, *Panurge und Hermes: zum Ursprung eines Charakters bei Rabelais* (Bonn: Romanisches Seminar, 1958), and the chapter entitled "Rabelais's Panurge," in Walter Kaiser's *Praisers of Folly* (Cambridge: Harvard University Press, 1963), pp. 191–92. See also the articles by Mario Roques, "Aspects de Panurge," in *François Rabelais: Ouvrage publié pour le quatrième centenaire de sa mort 1553–1953* (Geneva: Droz, 1953), pp. 120–30, and W. M. Frohock, "Panurge as Comic Character," *Yale French Studies*, no. 23 ("Humor"): 71–76.

13. This and the following passage are from *OCJ*, I, 303–5; trans. *JMC*, pp. 224–25.

14. We are not attempting to prove influence in this study. This is not possible without more extensive information, both biographical and historical. M. A. Screech and Ruth Calder confirm our findings on a specific point, however: Joubert never mentions the name of Rabelais in his *Traité du Ris*.

15. *OCJ*, I, 312; trans. *JMC*, p. 229.

16. *OCJ*, I, 332–33; trans. *JMC*, p. 243.

17. *OCJ*, II, 243; trans. *JMC*, p. 593.

18. *OCJ*, II, 49–50; trans. *JMC*, p. 462.

19. *OCL*, VI, 113, n. 3.

20. It would be interesting to analyze the Dindenault episode from the point of view of *la cheute*. The surprise ending that Rabelais gives it establishes the necessary element of chance.

21. *ER* 1: 176–78.

22. We recall the terrible punishment meted out to the *escholier Limosin* at the end of the sixth chapter of *Pantagruel*. See François Rigolot's analysis of this episode, *Les Langages de Rabelais* (Geneva: Droz, 1972), pp. 34–36.

23. *OCJ*, II, 54–55; trans. *JMC*, p. 465.

24. *OCJ*, II, 56; trans. *JMC*, p. 466.

25. M. A. Screech and Ruth Calder, "Some Renaissance Attitudes to Laughter," in *Humanism in France*, ed. A. H. T. Levi (London: Manchester University Press, 1970), p. 221.

26. This and the following passages from this episode are from *OCJ*, II, 58; trans. *JMC*, p. 467.

27. Frère Jan's added commentary is lacking in the 1548 edition (*dite partielle*). See *Le Quart Livre de Pantagruel*, ed. Jean Plattard (Paris: Champion, 1910), p. 81.

28. *OCL*, VI, 134, n. 39.

29. "Enfin il apparaît que l'on ne saurait trop se méfier de l'humour rabelaisien: il est tout aussi dangereux de croire Rabelais sur parole que de l'accuser d'erreur, dans son vocabulaire même, et cela n'avait, croyons-nous, jamais été jusqu'ici signalé, sauf pour d'évidents jeux de mot ou contrepèteries, il peut y avoir des contresens volontaires. L'humour est chez lui partout et c'est bien ce qui rend si difficile de pénétrer sa pensée profonde" (*ER* 1: 179).

30. See François Rigolot's discussion of this precise point (*Les Langages de Rabelais*, pp. 40–48). He stresses the importance of Pantagruel's presence in ultimately arresting the catastrophe to which other critics have alluded.

31. See Alfred Glauser's discussion of death in Rabelais (*Rabelais créateur*, pp. 72–76).

32. *OCJ*, I, 68–69; trans. *FG*, p. 22.

33. *OCL*, I, 158–60.

34. Cf. Arthur Koestler's remarks concerning the "child-adult" in *The Act of Creation* (New York: Macmillan, 1964), pp. 68–69.

Chapter Four

1. Henri Bergson, *Le Rire: Essai sur la signification du comique*, 273rd ed. (Paris: P. U. F., 1969), p. 79.

2. Starting with Kant (*Kritik der Urteilskraft*), theories of the comic emphasize more and more heavily the intellectual phases of the comic mechanism rather than the physiological effects that it has. See Max Eastman, *The Sense of Humor* (New York: Charles Scribner's Sons, 1922), pp. 130–31; J. Y. T. Greig, *The Psychology of Laughter and Comedy* (London: G. Allen & Unwin, 1923), appendix; Danilo

Romano, *Essai sur le comique de Molière* (Berne: Studiorum Romanicorum Collectio Turicensis, 1950), pp. 20–21; Robert Escarpit, *L'Humour* (Paris: P. U. F., 1967), pp. 11–12; Charles Mauron, *Psychocritique du genre comique* (Paris: Corti, 1964), appendix C; Arthur Koestler, *The Act of Creation,* (New York: Macmillan, 1964), pp. 27–32.

3. Joubert takes the term in the sense that it has in the *Rhetorica ad Herennium:* "the exposition of pertinent topics, deeds and events." See Lee A. Sonnino, *A Handbook to Sixteenth-Century Rhetoric* (New York: Barnes & Noble, 1968), p. 243.

4. Cf. M. A. Screech's article on this episode, "The Legal Comedy of Rabelais in the *Tiers Livre* of *Pantagruel,*" *ER* 5: 175–95.

5. This and the following passage are from *OCJ*, II, 152–54; trans. *JMC*, p. 531–32.

6. See Pierre-Paul Plan, *Les Editions de Rabelais de 1532 à 1711* (Paris: Imprimerie Nationale, 1904), p. 139, and *Le Quart Livre de Pantagruel*, ed. Jean Plattard (Paris: Champion, 1910), pp. i–v.

7. On the therapeutic value of Rabelais's work, see Georges Lote, *La Vie et l'oeuvre de François Rabelais* (Paris: Droz, 1938), pp. 57–59; Plattard, *François Rabelais* (Paris: Boivin, 1932), p. 120; Béatrix Ravà, *L'Art de Rabelais* (Rome: E. Loscher, 1910), pp. 115–35; Marcel Tetel, *Etude sur le comique de Rabelais* (Firenze: Olschki, 1966), p. 6; J. C. Powys, *Rabelais* (London: Bodley Head, 1948), and in his *Visions and Revisions* (New York: G. A. Shaw, 1915), pp. 25–34; Mikhail Bakhtin, *Rabelais and His World,* trans. H. Iswolsky (Cambridge: M. I. T. Press, 1968), p. 68; Thomas M. Greene, *Rabelais: A Study in Comic Courage* (Englewood Cliffs: Prentice-Hall, 1970), p. 84; Dorothy Gabe Coleman, *Rabelais: A Study in Prose Fiction* (Cambridge: University Press, 1971), pp. 202–03, 225.

8. *OCJ*, II, 3; trans. *JMC*, p. 435.

9. Jean Plattard, in his book *La Vie et l'oeuvre de Rabelais* (Paris: Boivin, 1939), pp. 116–19, makes a useful distinction between *devis* and *narrés:* the former are discursive whereas the latter are more dramatic.

10. *Aversio* (Apostrophe). Sonnino, *A Handbook to Sixteenth-Century Rhetoric,* pp. 33–34.

11. The passages in this episode are from *OCJ*, I, 51–54; trans. *JMC*, pp. 64–66.

12. The passages in this episode are from *OCJ*, II, 547; trans. *JMC*, p. 383. I do not agree with Cohen's attribution of this passage to Pantagruel. See *OCB*, 452, n. 1.

Chapter Five

1. *Dictionnaire de la langue française du seizième siècle,* vol. VI, ed. E. Huguet (Paris: E. Champion, 1925 to 1967), p. 490: "Faire des plaisanteries, dire des mots spirituels, remarquables."

2. *Dictionnaire alphabétique & analogique de la langue française,* ed. Paul Robert (Paris: Société du Nouveau Littré, 1970), p. 1513.

3. A. J. Greimas, *Dictionnaire de l'ancien français jusqu'au milieu du XIVe siècle* (Paris: Larousse, 1969), p. 552.

4. Cf. Marcel Tetel, *Etude sur le comique de Rabelais* (Firenze: Olschki, 1966), pp. 95, 138.

5. See Lee A. Sonnino's checklist (*A Handbook to Sixteenth-Century Rhetoric* [New York: Barnes & Noble, 1968], pp. 233–36) for rhetorical texts to which Joubert might have had access. He probably consulted Jules-César Scaliger's *Poetices libri septem* (Lyons: A. Vincent, 1561).

6. David Ross, *Aristotle* (London: Methuen, 1923), pp. 122, 143.

7. *OCJ,* I, 296; trans. *JMC,* p. 219.

8. Huguet, *Dictionnaire,* vol. VI, p. 666.

9. "qui happe tout, rifle tout, racle tout," as cited in Huguet, *Dictionnaire,* vol. VI, p. 667.

10. Ross, *Aristotle,* p. 167.

11. *OCJ,* I, 348; trans. *JMC,* p. 253.

12. Besides *lascif,* another meaning of the term in the sixteenth century was *complexe:* "qui s'étend en beaucoup de branches." Huguet, *Dictionnaire,* vol. IV, p. 776.

13. This and the following passages are from *OCJ,* I, 348; trans. *JMC,* p. 253.

14. One finds in fact several ideas commonly attributed to later comic theorists in Joubert's *Traité.*

15. *OCJ,* I, 74.

16. *OCJ,* II, 194; trans. *JMC,* p. 560.

17. The following definition of *emphase* given by Pierre Fabri, *Le Grand et vrai art de pleine Rhétorique,* 2 vols. (Rouen: A. Héron, 1889), 2: 193, is of particular interest here: "C'est quant dessoulz aulcun dict aultre sentence se peult entendre." What better example could be cited to demonstrate the ambiguity of terms and the imprecision in language in the sixteenth century?

18. *OCJ,* II, 200; trans. *JMC,* p. 564.

19. This and the following passages in this episode are from *OCJ,* I, 289; trans. *JMC,* p. 214.

20. This and the above passage are from *OCJ,* I, 502–3; trans. *JMC,* p. 354.

21. The passages in this episode are from *OCJ,* I, 153; trans. based upon *JMC,* p. 127.

22. *OCJ,* II, 155; trans. *JMC,* p. 553.

23. *OCJ,* II, 69; trans. *JMC,* pp. 474–75.

24. *OCJ,* I, 351–52; trans. *JMC,* p. 255.

25. Panurge's version is as follows: "'Il n'est umbre que de courtines, fumée que de tetins et clicquetys que de couillons.'" *OCJ,* I, 352. The translation is from

JMC, p. 255: "'There is no shade like that of curtains, no smoke like steaming breasts, and no clattering like the sound of ballocks.'"

26. The passages from this episode are from *OCJ*, II, 232–33; trans. *JMC*, p. 585.

27. Baudelaire speaks of laughter in the following terms: "Le rire est satanique, il est donc profondément humain. Il est dans l'homme la conséquence de sa propre supériorité; et, en effet, comme le rire est essentiellement contradictoire, c'est-à-dire qu'il est à la fois signe d'une grandeur infinie et d'une misère infinie relativement à l'Etre absolu dont il possède la conception, grandeur infinie relativement aux animaux. C'est du choc perpétuel de ces deux infinis que se dégage le rire." This passage is from "De l'essence du rire," in *Oeuvres complètes: Curiosités esthétiques*, ed. Jacques Crépet (Paris: Louis Conard, 1923), p. 379. See James S. Patty's article, "Baudelaire and Bossuet on Laughter," *PMLA* 80: 459–61.

28. It should be recalled that Aristotle admits the possibility of designating such concomitants as causes *per accidens*. Ross, *Aristotle*, p. 72.

Chapter Six

1. *OCJ*, I, 56; trans. *FG*, p. 2 and *JMC*, p. 37.
2. *OCJ*, I, 381; trans. *JMC*, p. 275.
3. *OCJ*, I, 24; trans. *FG*, p. 12.
4. *OCJ*, I, 33; trans. *JMC*, p. 53.
5. *OCJ*, I, 146–47; trans. *JMC*, p. 123.
6. *OCJ*, I, 22; trans. *JMC*, p. 48.
7. *OCJ*, I, 76; trans. *JMC*, p. 79.
8. *OCJ*, II, 239; trans. *JMC*, p. 591.
9. *OCJ*, II, 577.
10. *OCJ*, II, 11 and n. 2; trans. *JMC*, p. 439.
11. *OCJ*, I, 403; trans. *JMC*, p. 287. For the role of cruelty and anger in ancient laughter, see Mary Grant, *The Ancient Rhetorical Theories of the Laughable: The Greek Rhetoricians and Cicero*, University of Wisconsin Studies in Language and Literature, no. 21 (Madison: University Press, 1924).
12. This and the following passage are from *OCJ*, II, 199; trans. *JMC*, p. 564.
13. This and the above passage are from *OCJ*, II, 50–51; trans. *JLC*, pp. 521 and 523.
14. This and the following passage are from *OCJ*, II, 26; trans. *JMC*, pp. 447–48.
15. *OCJ*, I, 549; trans. *JMC*, p. 384.
16. This and the following passages in this episode are from *OCJ*, II, 109–12; trans. *JMC*, pp. 501–3.
17. Sigmund Freud, *Jokes and their Relation to the Unconscious*, trans. James Strachey (New York: Norton, 1960), and *The Interpretation of Dreams*, trans. A. A. Brill (New York: Macmillan, 1939).

Chapter Seven

1. *Aristotle: The Poetics; Longinus: On the Sublime; Demetrius: On Style,* ed. W. H. Fyfe, trans. W. R. Roberts, Loeb Classical Series (London and Cambridge, Mass.: W. Heinemann and Harvard Univ. Press, 1927), pp. x–xi. See also *The Great Critics,* ed. J. H. Smith and F. W. Parks (New York: Norton, 1951), p. 3.

2. See Gérard Defaux, *Pantagruel et les Sophistes: Contribution à l'histoire de l'humanisme chrétien au XVIe siècle* (The Hague: Nijhoff, 1973), for the importance of dialectics in Rabelais. The medieval *disputatio* is well covered in Louis Massevieau's *Colloques scolaires du XVIe siècle et leurs auteurs 1480–1570* (Paris: J. Bonhoure, 1878).

3. Jean Paris uses this term to explain the nature of Rabelaisian ambiguity: "C'est que l'ambiguité ne s'indique temporellement qu'en indiquant aussi son contraire: la disjonction." Narration necessitates the rhythmical progression of the opposing poles according to what the critic calls the "figure majeure: l'*alternance.*" *Rabelais au futur* (Paris: Seuil, 1970), p. 135. This *intuition fondamentale* accounts, according to Denis de Rougemont, for more than we realize in Western culture. He traces it back to Heraclitus. This notion finds expression in literary criticism in Albert Thibaudet, *Réflexions sur la critique* (Paris: Gallimard, 1939), esp. p. 46.

4. Much as will Nicolas de Nancel in his *Analogia Microcosmi ad microcosmon . . . ,* published by his brother Pierre (Paris: C. Morelli, 1611).

5. The *dizain,* we recall, appeared for the first time in 1534 with the third edition of *Pantagruel.* See Pierre-Paul Plan, *Les Editions de Rabelais de 1532 à 1711* (Paris: Imprimerie Nationale, 1904), pp. 50–51. See also Gérard Defaux's remarks concerning this particular edition of *Pantagruel,* in "Rabelais et les cloches de Notre Dame," *ER* 9: 1–28, esp. p. 16, n. 77.

6. *OCJ,* I, 213; trans. *JMC,* p. 166.

7. *OCJ,* I, 232; trans. *FG,* p. 77.

8. Floyd Gray, "Ambiguity and Point of View in the Prologue to *Gargantua,*" *RR* 56: 12–21.

9. Defaux, "Rabelais et les cloches de Notre Dame."

10. *OCJ,* I, 5; trans. *FG,* p. 1.

11. Most of these translations are from *JMC.*

12. *OCJ,* I, 111; trans. *FG,* p. 51.

13. *OCJ,* I, 48; trans. *FG,* p. 16.

14. See *ER* 11, in which four of the twelve articles deal with the publication date of the *princeps* edition of *Gargantua.*

15. This is the text of the 1532 edition as found reproduced photographically in *Pantagruel,* ed. V.-L. Saulnier (Paris: Seuil, 1962), p. 7. The typographical transcription of this entire prologue is in Charles Brunet's *Recherches bibliographiques et critiques sur les éditions originales des cinq livres du roman satirique de Rabelais . . .* (Paris: P. Jannet, 1852), pp. 16–19. The translation is from *FG,* pp. 71–72.

16. This and the following passages are taken from *OCJ*, I, 216–17; trans. *FG*, p. 72.

17. Raymond Lebègue, *Rabelais* (Tübingen: Max Niemeyer Verlag, 1952), p. 14.

18. *OCJ*, I, 67; trans. *JMC*, p. 73.

19. Paris, *Rabelais au futur*, p. 135.

20. This and the following passages in this episode are from *OCJ*, I, 232–33; trans. *FG*, pp. 77–78.

21. Paris, *Rabelais au futur*, pp. 133–63.

22. "L'art de la composition consistera à mettre en valeur les deux faces du sujet, la face populaire et la face savante." Pierre Villey, *Marot et Rabelais* (Paris: Champion, 1923), p. 155. Our translation.

23. Villey, *Marot et Rabelais*, p. 249.

24. Ibid., p. 248.

25. Ibid., p. 257.

26. *OCJ*, I, 418–19; trans. *JMC*, p. 298.

27. Villey, *Marot et Rabelais* p. 257. V.-L. Saulnier also suggests this sort of reversal between the *Pantagruel-Gargantua* and the *Tiers-Quart Livre*, in "Pantagruel et sa famille de mots," *L'Information Littéraire* 12: 47–57.

28. Northrop Frye, *Anatomy of Criticism* (Princeton: Princeton University Press, 1957), pp. 223–39. This passage is cited in Michel Beaujour, *Le Jeu de Rabelais* (Paris: L'Herne, 1969), p. 110.

29. Marcel Tetel, *Etude sur le comique de Rabelais* (Firenze: Olschki, 1966), p. 138.

30. *OCJ*, I, 555–56; trans. *JMC*, p. 389.

31. Cf. Ludwig Schrader, *Panurge und Hermes: zum Ursprung eines Charakters bei Rabelais* (Bonn: Romanisches Seminar, 1958), and Barbara C. Bowen, *The Age of Bluff: Paradox and Ambiguity in Rabelais and Montaigne* (Urbana: University of Illinois Press, 1972), pp. 82–83.

32. This and the following passage are from *OCJ*, I, 463–64; trans. *JMC*, pp. 327–28.

33. *OCJ*, I, 474; trans. *JMC*, p. 335.

34. *OCJ*, I, 570.

35. Bowen, *The Age of Bluff*, pp. 83–84.

36. Alfred Glauser, *Rabelais créateur* (Paris: Nizet, 1966), p. 40.

37. Bowen, *The Age of Bluff*, pp. 93–94.

38. This and the above passage are from *OCJ*, II, 65–66; trans. *JMC*, p. 472.

39. *OCJ*, II, 125; trans. *JMC*, pp. 511–12.

40. *OCJ*, II, 60; trans. *JMC*, p. 468.

41. *Le Quart Livre de Pantagruel*, ed. Jean Plattard (Paris: Champion, 1910), p. 165.

42. *OCJ*, II, 93; trans. *JMC*, p. 490.

43. *OCJ*, II, 104; trans. *JMC*, p. 498.

44. *Le Quart Livre de Pantagruel*, p. 165.

45. Albert-Marie Schmidt, "La Littérature humaniste à l'époque de la Renaissance," in *Histoire des littératures*, 3 vols., Encyclopédie de la Pléiade, 7 (Paris: Bibliothèque de la Pléiade, 1967), 3: 167.

46. *OCJ*, II, 3; trans. *JMC*, p. 435.

47. Marcel De Grève, *L'Interprétation de Rabelais au XVIe siècle* (Geneva: Droz, 1961), p. 60.

48. *OCJ*, I, xl: "Rabelais, quoi qu'il prétende, n'a pas écrit que pour les *'beuveurs tres illustres'* et les *'verolez tres precieux.'* L'intelligence de son oeuvre n'est plus accessible à tous aujourd'hui surtout où la connaissance du latin manque à plus d'un lecteur."

49. It has been proven scientifically that Erasmus suffered from syphilis. See the editor's article "Desiderius Erasmus (1466–1536): The Great Humanist," *Journal of the American Medical Association* 210: 1587–88.

50. For a more thorough treatment of Ficino's revival of Platonic doctrines during the Renaissance, see Ernst Cassirer's *The Individual and the Cosmos in Renaissance Philosophy,* trans. Mario Domandi (New York: Harper Torchbooks, 1963). See also Paul Oskar Kristeller, *Renaissance Thought: The Classic, Scholastic, and Humanistic Strains,* rev. and enlarged ed. (New York: Harper Torchbooks, 1955; 1961), pp. 48–69.

51. Two critics in particular have given expression to this idea. François Rigolot, in *Les Langages de Rabelais,* has concluded that the author's preoccupation with both the problematical nature and the poetic quality of language itself accounts for the "double tension" that is the *qualité première* of the work's seething expression. Jean-Yves Pouilloux in his article "Notes sur deux chapitres du *Quart Livre* LX–LXI," *Littérature* 5: 88–94, shows the simultaneous presence of two different systems of presentation in the *paroles gelées* episode. One is proper to the work as a whole, working toward the unfolding of the *roman,* and the other, proper only to the episode itself, functions as a pause in the first system and at the same time develops a closed presentation within the two chapter *escale.* This contradiction, maintains Pouilloux, is characteristic of all of Rabelais.

52. "Si le style est la pointe qui écrit, on peut l'imaginer chez lui comme les mouvements d'un fleuret. . . . Tout l'être est intéressé dans l'acte d'écrire: une escrime invisible se dessine dans l'oeuvre, un mouvement ensorcelé où tout un monde agit, frappe, saute et danse." Glauser, *Rabelais créateur,* pp. 16 and 141. Our translation. See also Dorothy Gabe Coleman's remarks concerning the *Pantagruel* in *Rabelais: A Study in Prose Fiction* (Cambridge: University Press, 1971), p. 224.

53. *OCJ*, II, 23; trans. *JMC*, p. 446.

54. Glauser, *Rabelais créateur*, pp. 157 and 186.

55. "Car l'objet littéraire est une étrange toupie, qui n'existe qu'en mouvement. Pour la faire surgir, il faut un acte concret qui s'appelle la lecture, et elle ne dure qu'autant que cette lecture peut durer." Jean-Paul Sartre, *Qu'est-ce que la littérature?* (Paris: Gallimard, 1948), p. 52. Our translation.

56. Floyd Gray, "Ambiguity and Point of View in the Prologue to *Gargantua*," *RR* 56: 12–21.

57. See Stanley G. Eskin's article, in which he lists the French critics who have sought to distinguish Rabelais's light moods from his serious ones, "Mythic Unity in Rabelais," *PMLA* 79: 88–94. Henri Busson, however, has spoken of the difficulty of separating them: *Le Rationalisme dans la littérature de la Renaissance* (Paris: Vrin, 1957), pp. 157–78. See also Paul Naudon's discussions, "Le Dualisme de Rabelais" and "L'Esprit de Synthèse" in his book, *Rabelais Franc-maçon* (Paris: La Balance, 1954), pp. 60–64.

58. *OCJ*, I, 3; trans. *JMC*, p. 36.

Conclusions

1. This and the above passage are from *OCJ*, II, 11–14; trans. *JLC*, pp. 495–97.

2. *OCJ*, I, 411; trans. *JMC*, p. 293.

3. For the switching of the levels of discourse in Rabelais, see Floyd Gray's recent book, *Rabelais et l'écriture* (Paris: Nizet, 1974).

4. Gérard Genette, "Raisons de la critique pure," in *Les Chemins actuels de la critique*, ed. Georges Poulet et al. (Paris: Union Générale, 1968), pp. 125–41, esp. p. 139.

5. Arthur Koestler, *The Act of Creation* (New York: Macmillan, 1964), pp. 1–69. See also his *Insight and Outlook* (Lincoln: University of Nebraska Press, 1949).

6. Doctor Guy Godlewski has written the following on the importance of anatomy in Rabelais's time: "Aussi n'est-il pas surprenant que François Rabelais ... se tourne ... vers l'anatomie qui, pour un esprit du XVIe siècle, constitue la suprême curiosité et où réside, croit-on, la clef des problèmes de la vie." His article, "Rabelais à Montpellier," is in his *Rabelais écrivain-médecin* (Paris: Garance, 1959), pp. 29–41. At least two other articles in this publication relate to our subject: Doctor Olivier Loras's "Vers une psychanalyse de Rabelais," pp. 237–50, and Doctor Ludovic O'Followell's "L'Humour dans Rabelais," pp. 213–18.

7. M. A. Screech, *The Rabelaisian Marriage: Aspects of Rabelais' Religion, Ethics & Comic Philosophy* (London: E. Arnold, 1958), p. 25.

8. Rosalie Colie, *Paradoxia Epidemica* (Princeton: Princeton University Press, 1966), pp. 518–19.

9. Floyd Gray, "Structure and Meaning in the Prologue to the *Tiers Livre*," *L'Esprit Créateur* 3: 57–62.

Select Bibliography

Bakhtin, Mikhail. *Rabelais and His World.* trans. H. Iswolsky. Cambridge: M.I.T. Press, 1968.

Beaujour, Michel. *Le Jeu de Rabelais.* Paris: L'Herne, 1969.

Bowen, Barbara C. *The Age of Bluff: Paradox and Ambiguity in Rabelais and Montaigne.* Urbana: University of Illinois Press, 1972.

Butor, Michel, and Denis Hollier. *Rabelais ou c'était pour rire.* Paris: Larousse, 1972.

Defaux, Gérard. *Pantagruel et les Sophistes: Contribution à l'histoire de l'humanisme chrétien au XVIe siècle.* The Hague: Nijhoff, 1973.

De Grève, Marcel. *L'Interprétation de Rabelais au XVIe siècle.* Geneva: Droz, 1961.

Glauser, Alfred. *Rabelais créateur.* Paris: Nizet, 1966.

Gray, Floyd. *Rabelais et l'écriture.* Paris: Nizet, 1974.

Greene, Thomas M. *Rabelais: A Study in Comic Courage.* Englewood Cliffs: Prentice-Hall, 1970.

Paris, Jean. *Rabelais au futur.* Paris: Seuil, 1970.

Plattard, Jean. *L'Oeuvre de Rabelais (Sources, Invention et Composition).* Paris: Champion, 1910.

Rigolot, François. *Les Langages de Rabelais.* Geneva: Droz, 1972.

Screech, M. A. *The Rabelaisian Marriage: Aspects of Rabelais' Religion, Ethics & Comic Philosophy.* London: E. Arnold, 1958.

Spitzer, Leo. "Rabelais et les 'rabelaisants.'" *Studi Francesi* 4 (1960): 401–23.

Tetel, Marcel. *Etude sur le comique de Rabelais.* Firenze: Olschki, 1966.

Index